EARLY CHILDHOOD E

SHARON RYA

Leading for Change in Early Care and Education: Cultivating Leadership from Within
ANNE L. DOUGLASS

When Pre-K Comes to School: Policy, Partnerships, and the Early Childhood Education Workforce
BETHANY WILINSKI

Young Investigators: The Project Approach in the Early Years, 3rd Ed.
JUDY HARRIS HELM & LILIAN G. KATZ

Continuity in Children's Worlds: Choices and Consequences for Early Childhood Settings
MELISSA M. JOZWIAK, BETSY J. CAHILL, & RACHEL THEILHEIMER

The Early Intervention Guidebook for Families and Professionals: Partnering for Success, 2nd Ed.
BONNIE KEILTY

STEM Learning with Young Children: Inquiry Teaching with Ramps and Pathways
SHELLY COUNSELL, LAWRENCE ESCALADA, ROSEMARY GEIKEN, MELISSA SANDER, JILL UHLENBERG, BETH VAN MEETEREN, SONIA YOSHIZAWA, & BETTY ZAN

Courageous Leadership in Early Childhood Education: Taking a Stand for Social Justice
SUSI LONG, MARIANA SOUTO-MANNING, & VIVIAN MARIA VASQUEZ, EDS.

Teaching Kindergarten: Learner-Centered Classrooms for the 21st Century
JULIE DIAMOND, BETSY GROB, & FRETTA REITZES, EDS.

Healthy Learners: A Whole Child Approach to Reducing Disparities in Early Education
ROBERT CROSNOE, CLAUDE BONAZZO, & NINA WU

The New Early Childhood Professional: A Step-by-Step Guide to Overcoming Goliath
VALORA WASHINGTON, BRENDA GADSON, & KATHRYN L. AMEL

Eight Essential Techniques for Teaching with Intention: What Makes Reggio and Other Inspired Approaches Effective
ANN LEWIN-BENHAM

Teaching and Learning in a Diverse World, 4th Ed.
PATRICIA G. RAMSEY

In the Spirit of the Studio: Learning from the *Atelier* of Reggio Emilia, 2nd Ed.
LELLA GANDINI, LYNN HILL, LOUISE CADWELL, & CHARLES SCHWALL, EDS.

Leading Anti-Bias Early Childhood Programs: A Guide for Change
LOUISE DERMAN-SPARKS, DEBBIE LEEKEENAN, & JOHN NIMMO

Exploring Mathematics Through Play in the Early Childhood Classroom
AMY NOELLE PARKS

Becoming Young Thinkers: Deep Project Work in the Classroom
JUDY HARRIS HELM

The Early Years Matter: Education, Care, and the Well-Being of Children, Birth to 8
MARILOU HYSON & HEATHER BIGGAR TOMLINSON

Thinking Critically About Environments for Young Children: Bridging Theory and Practice
LISA P. KUH, ED.

Standing Up for Something Every Day: Ethics and Justice in Early Childhood Classrooms
BEATRICE S. FENNIMORE

FirstSchool: Transforming PreK–3rd Grade for African American, Latino, and Low-Income Children
SHARON RITCHIE & LAURA GUTMANN, EDS.

The States of Child Care: Building a Better System
SARA GABLE

Early Childhood Education for a New Era: Leading for Our Profession
STACIE G. GOFFIN

Everyday Artists: Inquiry and Creativity in the Early Childhood Classroom
DANA FRANTZ BENTLEY

Multicultural Teaching in the Early Childhood Classroom: Approaches, Strategies, and Tools, Preschool–2nd Grade
MARIANA SOUTO-MANNING

Inclusion in the Early Childhood Classroom: What Makes a Difference?
SUSAN L. RECCHIA & YOON-JOO LEE

Language Building Blocks: Essential Linguistics for Early Childhood Educators
ANITA PANDEY

Understanding the Language Development and Early Education of Hispanic Children
EUGENE E. GARCÍA & ERMINDA H. GARCÍA

To look for other titles in this series, visit www.tcpress.com

continued

Moral Classrooms, Moral Children: Creating a Constructivist Atmosphere in Early Education, 2nd Ed.
RHETA DEVRIES & BETTY ZAN

Defending Childhood
BEVERLY FALK, ED.

Don't Leave the Story in the Book
MARY HYNES-BERRY

Starting with Their Strengths
DEBORAH C. LICKEY & DENISE J. POWERS

The Play's the Thing
ELIZABETH JONES & GRETCHEN REYNOLDS

Twelve Best Practices for Early Childhood Education
ANN LEWIN-BENHAM

Big Science for Growing Minds
JACQUELINE GRENNON BROOKS

What If All the Kids Are White? 2nd Ed.
LOUISE DERMAN-SPARKS & PATRICIA G. RAMSEY

Seen and Heard
ELLEN LYNN HALL & JENNIFER KOFKIN RUDKIN

Supporting Boys' Learning
BARBARA SPRUNG, MERLE FROSCHL, & NANCY GROPPER

Young English Language Learners
EUGENE E. GARCÍA & ELLEN C. FREDE, EDS.

Connecting Emergent Curriculum and Standards in the Early Childhood Classroom
SYDNEY L. SCHWARTZ & SHERRY M. COPELAND

Infants and Toddlers at Work
ANN LEWIN-BENHAM

The View from the Little Chair in the Corner
CINDY RZASA BESS

Culture and Child Development in Early Childhood Programs
CAROLLEE HOWES

The Story in the Picture
CHRISTINE MULCAHEY

Educating and Caring for Very Young Children, 2nd Ed.
DORIS BERGEN, REBECCA REID, & LOUIS TORELLI

Beginning School
RICHARD M. CLIFFORD & GISELE M. CRAWFORD, EDS.

Emergent Curriculum in the Primary Classroom
CAROL ANNE WIEN, ED.

Enthusiastic and Engaged Learners
MARILOU HYSON

Powerful Children
ANN LEWIN-BENHAM

The Early Care and Education Teaching Workforce at the Fulcrum
SHARON LYNN KAGAN, KRISTIE KAUERZ, & KATE TARRANT

Windows on Learning, 2nd Ed.
JUDY HARRIS HELM, SALLEE BENEKE, & KATHY STEINHEIMER

Ready or Not
STACIE G. GOFFIN & VALORA WASHINGTON

Supervision in Early Childhood Education, 3rd Ed.
JOSEPH J. CARUSO WITH M. TEMPLE FAWCETT

Guiding Children's Behavior
EILEEN S. FLICKER & JANET ANDRON HOFFMAN

The War Play Dilemma, 2nd Ed.
DIANE E. LEVIN & NANCY CARLSSON-PAIGE

Possible Schools
ANN LEWIN-BENHAM

Everyday Goodbyes
NANCY BALABAN

Playing to Get Smart
ELIZABETH JONES & RENATTA M. COOPER

How to Work with Standards in the Early Childhood Classroom
CAROL SEEFELDT

Understanding Assessment and Evaluation in Early Childhood Education, 2nd Ed.
DOMINIC F. GULLO

The Emotional Development of Young Children, 2nd Ed.
MARILOU HYSON

Effective Partnering for School Change
JIE-QI CHEN ET AL.

Young Children Continue to Reinvent Arithmetic—2nd Grade, 2nd Ed.
CONSTANCE KAMII

Bringing Learning to Life
LOUISE BOYD CADWELL

The Colors of Learning
ROSEMARY ALTHOUSE, MARGARET H. JOHNSON, & SHARON T. MITCHELL

A Matter of Trust
CAROLLEE HOWES & SHARON RITCHIE

Embracing Identities in Early Childhood Education
SUSAN GRIESHABER & GAILE S. CANNELLA, EDS.

Bambini: The Italian Approach to Infant/Toddler Care
LELLA GANDINI & CAROLYN POPE EDWARDS, EDS.

Serious Players in the Primary Classroom, 2nd Ed.
SELMA WASSERMANN

Young Children Reinvent Arithmetic, 2nd Ed.
CONSTANCE KAMII

Bringing Reggio Emilia Home
LOUISE BOYD CADWELL

LEADING for CHANGE
in Early Care and Education

CULTIVATING LEADERSHIP from WITHIN

Anne L. Douglass Foreword by Lea J. E. Austin

TEACHERS COLLEGE PRESS
TEACHERS COLLEGE | COLUMBIA UNIVERSITY
NEW YORK AND LONDON

Published by Teachers College Press, 1234 Amsterdam Avenue, New York, NY 10027

Cover photos (top to bottom, left to right): mheim3011, zdenkam, XiXinXing, yongtick, diego_cervo, m-imagephotography, m-imagephotography, ajr_images, jacoblund, m-imagephotography, szefei, pablocalvog, champja, m-imagephotography, m-imagephotography, m-imagephotography, monkeybusinessimages, szefei, m-imagephotography , Szepy, monkeybusinessimages, all from iStock by Getty Images.

Library of Congress Cataloging-in-Publication Data

Names: Douglass, Anne, author.
Title: Leading for change in early care and education : cultivating leadership from within / Anne L. Douglass ; foreword by Lea J.E. Austin.
Description: New York, NY : Teachers College Press, 2017. | Series: Early childhood education series | Includes bibliographical references and index.
Identifiers: LCCN 2017023615 (print) | LCCN 2017035757 (ebook) | ISBN 9780807776520 (ebook) | ISBN 9780807758366 (hardcover : alk. paper) | ISBN 9780807758359 (pbk. : alk. paper)
Subjects: LCSH: Early childhood educators—Professional relationships—United States. | Early childhood education--United States. | Educational change—United States. | Educational leadership—United States.
Classification: LCC LB1775.6 (ebook) | LCC LB1775.6 .D68 2017 (print) | DDC 372.21—dc23
LC record available at https://lccn.loc.gov/2017023615

ISBN 978-0-8077-5835-9 (paper)
ISBN 978-0-8077-5836-6 (hardcover)
ISBN 978-0-8077-7652-0 (ebook)

Printed on acid-free paper
Manufactured in the United States of America

24 23 22 21 20 19 18 17 8 7 6 5 4 3 2 1

Contents

Foreword

Anne Douglass has written a book that calls attention to and offers a pathway for perhaps the greatest, yet least visible, challenge facing the early care and education field today: the leadership development gap. Without a cadre of diverse leaders who can envision an early care and education system that works for all children and for early educators, efforts to improve the system will continue to be stymied.

Early care and education has increasingly entered the public domain with its promise to deliver long-lasting benefits for children and society. Yet efforts to transform early care and education so that it can deliver on its promise for all children continue to fall short. Today, there is no shortage of policymakers, economists, researchers, and activists offering strategies to expand and strengthen the availability of high-quality early care and education services. Many of these well-intentioned strategies are focused on inputs and benchmarks designed to in some way change and measure those most intimately involved in, and as Douglass convincingly argues, most knowledgeable about, early care and education—early educators. But where are the early educators when these strategies are designed and implemented? Would strategies and solutions look different if educators themselves were the architects of change? Douglass makes a compelling case that the answer to this question is a resounding Yes. "All too often, early educators have been seen as the objects of change, rather than the architects and co-creators of change."

Perhaps because she has herself been an early educator, Douglass clearly recognizes that early educators are in possession of knowledge that is essential for informing change. But disturbingly, many of those leading change in early care and education today do not respect this knowledge or the holders of it. In no other comparative field do we see the most knowledgeable actors excluded from formal and informal leadership and change efforts. Yet in early care and education, it is unusual (rather than the norm) to find leadership development programs or an articulated pathway to leadership. Instead, we have what Douglass identifies as a leadership development gap. This does not mean that people are not filling leadership roles, sitting on committees, or having a voice in reform efforts. What it does mean, however, is that we have allowed a situation to fester in which those who most intimately understand the developmental and educational needs of children, and who understand the demands and challenges of delivering quality early care and learning, are at the greatest distance from filling leadership roles and driving change.

This gap is not insignificant or inconsequential. We should all take note that 40% of early educators are women of color, but the available evidence on those serving in formal leadership roles suggests that the leadership ranks are far less diverse. The lack of a pathway and environment that nurtures the development of leadership among early educators only serves to reinforce the status quo. We must be bold and declare this leadership gap and maintenance of the status quo to be unacceptable. This gap interferes with our ability to enact meaningful, systemic change, and Douglass boldly calls for a re-envisioning of access to leadership in early care and education.

Leading for Change in Early Care and Education: Cultivating Leadership from Within demonstrates the urgency for developing leadership from among the ranks of educators. Most importantly, and unlike most of the (albeit limited) texts that have called for leadership development in the field, this book steps beyond the call and offers a foundation and pathway for closing the leadership development gap. Douglass notes that traditional approaches and attributes associated with leadership—often hierarchical and stereotypically male—have not served the field well and are out of step with early care and education. Instead, she draws on the most current and rich theories and evidence about leading for change and developing leaders from within a given profession—those that are based on relationships and on a culture of innovation and improvement. Central to the leadership framework Douglass presents is the recognition that the expertise and experiences of the main actor in the field—the early educator—must be elevated, respected, and central to driving change. In my work with my colleagues at the Center for the Study of Child Care Employment, in which we survey teaching staff in part as a way to bring their voices to policymakers and other stakeholders, we are continuously struck by how eager early educators are to participate in our studies—for many, it's one of the few opportunities they've had to lend their voice to quality improvement processes. Rather than being an exception, educator voices should be the norm throughout all levels of the field.

Importantly, Douglass's book is more than a theoretical exercise. Her call for a paradigm shift in our understanding of who can and should lead, as well as a shift in our approaches to leadership and systems that nurture and promote early educator leadership, reflect lived experiences—her own as well as a cadre of leaders that she has helped to develop. Through the implementation of an innovative leadership development program she founded at the University of Massachusetts, Douglass guided her students—all working early educators—to combine the theories of leadership and change with their own practical experience and expertise in order to enact change. The results, chronicled in the later chapters of the book, are powerful and manyfold, not the least of which is a working model for advancing a systemic approach to closing the leadership development gap, and which encompasses both formal and informal systems of preparation and opportunity.

Should you find yourself wondering why attending to leadership in early care and education is such an urgent matter, or why an approach like Douglass's should be widely undertaken, I challenge you to envision, as I have and as Douglass has, what early care and education policies and services would look like if the educators themselves were leading the charge. As Douglass poses: "What if we believed that early educators could drive change to improve ECE? What would we do differently" to ensure and nurture their capacity to lead?

—Lea J. E. Austin, Ed.D., co-director,
Center for the Study of Child Care Employment,
University of California, Berkeley

Preface

High-quality early care and education is essential for children's healthy development and school readiness. Yet too few children and families have access to the quality care and early learning experiences that matter most. This is a pivotal moment in the development of the early care and education (ECE) profession for accelerating improvement and innovation to advance the field. Professional, government, and philanthropic groups all have major initiatives under way to improve ECE quality and strengthen the workforce; however, a focus on leadership development—engaging early educators as change agents—is missing from most of the current approaches to advancing the field.

Leadership is the next frontier in ECE. This book argues that leadership is an essential and untapped lever for change, with the potential to transform opportunities and outcomes for young children and their families. Early educators have unique expertise and knowledge from their daily interactions and relationships with young children and families. Any effort to effect change must tap into and elevate that expertise to inform and drive improvement and innovation. While holding great promise, leadership for change is a relatively unexplored, invisible, yet crucial dimension of the field. Few opportunities or systems exist to develop and support leadership from within the ECE workforce. All too often, early educators have been seen as the objects of change, rather than the architects and co-creators of change.

In this book, I adopt a definition of *leadership* as a process of influencing change in order to achieve a shared goal. Leaders engage in the process of driving change to achieve a positive, desired outcome. Leadership can be exercised by individuals and groups at all levels, regardless of formal titles or roles (Fletcher, 2004; Gittell & Douglass, 2012). Early education leaders can make a lasting difference in the lives of children and families. But for decades now the early care and education field repeatedly has identified the need for substantially increased attention to leadership development (Goffin, 2013; Kagan & Bowman, 1997). What is still missing is an intentional and deliberate system in ECE for cultivating, supporting, and nurturing the leadership of early educators.

My goal is to unleash the possibilities of leadership within the field, from the development of individual leaders, to leadership in teams and programs, to a field-wide ecosystem that cultivates and nurtures leaders. Getting real about early educator leadership—what it looks like, why it matters, and how we strengthen it—is the major contribution of this book. Many have called for leadership from within the field, but as of yet we have not systematically established a set of concrete steps for getting there, for helping our field and others see what it looks like or how to do it.

I am speaking to many audiences: educators, students, and all those who design, implement, and study programs and policies to support the ECE workforce and strengthen quality. I offer a research-based, theory-driven framework for developing and nurturing innovative, entrepreneurial, and skilled early educator leaders to drive transformative change—from classrooms and home-based programs to communities and beyond. Further, I call for a leadership development ecosystem that has the capacity to cultivate the leadership needed to address the challenge and transformative opportunity that we face.

ACKNOWLEDGMENTS

This book is dedicated to all of the early educators whom I've had the privilege to teach and work alongside over the past 25 years. I am especially grateful to the graduates of my Leadership and Change course at UMass Boston. These smart, creative, caring, and passionate early childhood educators inspired me to write this book. Their relentless pursuit of a better world for young children and families is a force for hope and transformative change, and a story that must be told. Over the years I have been blessed with many mentors, wise colleagues, partners, and collaborators who helped shape the ideas that became this book, including Sister Margaret Leonard at Project Hope in Boston, Lynne Mendes at UMass Boston, Jen Agosti at JRA Consulting, Gina Scaramella at the Boston Area Rape Crisis Center, Jody Hoffer Gittell at Brandeis University, Kim Syman at New Profit, and most recently Banu Özkazanç-Pan at UMass Boston. They have influenced me in immeasurable ways and have my deepest gratitude. I am equally grateful to my whole family for their support, patience, and ongoing feedback on this book, and to my parents, Jane and Gordon Douglass, who planted the seeds of social and economic justice and educational opportunity.

CHAPTER 1

Developing Leadership Within

The Next Frontier of Early Care and Education

High-quality early care and education helps children grow, learn, and thrive. This is true across the ECE mixed-delivery system that includes family child care, Head Start, center-based child care, and school-based preschool programs. Quality ECE enhances early learning and school readiness and helps prevent opportunity and achievement gaps (Shonkoff & Phillips, 2000). Leading economists tout ECE as one of the best public investments, with a high return on investment and a proven track record of promoting community and economic development and vitality (Heckman, 2012). Expectations are high for the long-lasting benefits of early care and education.

However, while the benefits for young children and families depend on the quality of the education they receive, many ECE programs do not have access to the resources needed to reach recognized thresholds for high quality. Moreover, research shows disturbing inequities in children's access to quality ECE. For example, a nationally representative study reported that African American children received the lowest-quality ECE (Hillemeier, Morgan, Farkas, & Maczuga, 2013). The most widely used criteria for defining quality include accreditation standards of the National Association for the Education of Young Children and the National Association for Family Child Care, states' Quality Rating and Improvement Systems (QRIS) standards, and the most recognized measures of classroom quality, such as the Environmental Rating Scales (Harms, Cryer, & Clifford, 2005, 2007). Reaching these benchmarks has been a persistent challenge, limiting the potential for ECE to deliver on its promise (Adams, Tout, & Zaslow, 2007; Pianta, Cox, & Snow, 2007; Tout, Epstein, Soli, & Lowe, 2015; Wesley & Buysse, 2010). The reasons for this persistent problem are complex. One key reason is the subject of this book: the leadership development gap in early care and education. This chapter describes the challenges and the opportunity for strengthening our field through the leadership of early educators. It introduces the research and theoretical foundations for this book's solution to the leadership development and quality gaps.

THE PROBLEM

The dearth of attention paid to leadership in ECE undermines the field's capacity to design and deliver the care that makes a difference for children and families most in need. Almost no systems exist to develop and support ECE leadership (Goffin, 2013; Wise & Wright, 2012). Low compensation continues to undermine the field, in both supporting and retaining experienced educators and leaders. Limited resources in ECE tend to go to direct services or entry-level workforce development, without addressing the systemic issues that keep us from ensuring that all young children have access to high-quality early learning and care.

Professional development and quality improvement systems can be designed to promote the leadership of early educators in order to drive changes in practice, but currently they fail to do so. We have not yet applied the deep body of evidence from improvement science about what it takes to make measurable and sustained improvements in quality. In addition, relational organizational science documents the profound ways in which workplace relationships influence a wide range of organizational outcomes. Yet this science also has not been widely applied in ECE. These are missed opportunities.

We have long known from other sectors, such as healthcare and K–12 education, that effective leadership at all levels is a key ingredient for achieving positive outcomes (Berwick, 1994). The recently released Institute of Medicine report on transforming the ECE workforce acknowledges the importance of leadership and calls for leadership development as one of its 13 recommendations (Institute of Medicine & National Research Council, 2015).

Unlike many other professionals, experienced early educators lack opportunities to grow throughout their careers and to develop the skills and supports they need to lead in their classrooms, organizations, communities, and beyond (Ramgopal, Dieterle, Aviles, McCreedy, & Davis, 2009; Taba et al., 1999). Investments in the teaching workforce are diminished when early childhood programs lack experienced leaders at all levels to support and retain good teachers and promote a culture of continuous quality improvement. Failing to nurture leadership from within can drive experienced and innovative thinkers from a field and interfere with the potential to deliver on its promise.

THE TRANSFORMATIVE OPPORTUNITY

Diverse, skilled, and creative leaders within the field are essential drivers of the transformative change urgently needed in ECE now. The scale of the ECE field and of its potential leadership impact is immense. Today, most children in the United States under the age of 5 are cared for in ECE settings, such

Foundational Building Blocks

- the science of change and improvement
- relational leadership and relational organizational science
- entrepreneurial leadership and innovation

as child care, preschool, family child care, Head Start and Early Head Start, and early childhood programs in public schools. Many children are cared for in ECE 40 to 50 hours a week, often over a period of several years. Early educators constitute 30% of the entire U.S. instructional workforce from early childhood to postsecondary education (National Research Council, 2012). They are the most racially, ethnically, and linguistically diverse sector of the education workforce from birth to postsecondary education. The diversity of this workforce is an asset, and cultivating diverse leadership is essential to the future of the field.

For the field to fulfill its mission and potential, it needs a bold new approach to leadership development. What will it take to develop this leadership? For the past 8 years, I have been studying innovations in ECE quality improvement and professional development, and designing models that operate from a set of assumptions different from those of "business as usual." Some might consider them *"disruptive innovations"* (Christensen, Johnson, & Horn, 2008)—a term used to characterize innovations that offer an alternative to the existing way of doing things, often by challenging the status quo. These innovations target gaps or offer something that may not yet be offered as a solution to a problem, either persistent or new. These models may be new in the ECE sector, but they have roots in sectors and disciplines where these approaches are more developed and widely used. These models are now being adapted and tested in ECE in ways that are strengthening leadership for change.

WHAT TO EXPECT IN THIS BOOK

Developing leadership from within our field is an untapped lever for transforming the ECE landscape, strengthening our workforce, and ensuring that all young children and their families thrive. This book applies a multidisciplinary lens to examine theory and research on leadership, change, improvement, and innovation. Rooted in this transdisciplinary analysis, it offers a new way of thinking about how ECE can—and must—cultivate a culture of diverse, innovative, and entrepreneurial leadership. It delves into this solution with a focus on three foundational building blocks, each supported by a rich body of evidence and theory from across disciplines.

Each of these components is explored in one Part of the book. The first Part presents the research and theoretical foundation, the second gives in-depth examples of how new leadership pathways are being tested and used, and the third proposes a new leadership development ecosystem for ECE.

The Research Foundations of Leadership for Change

New research and theory emerging in the relational and positive organizational sciences offers important evidence and insights about how to promote positive change and improve quality. Positive relationships, characterized by mutual respect and shared power, are key ingredients for successful change and improvement.

In the past, management science may have failed to offer relevant insights for the highly relationship-based context of ECE and similar human services sectors. What could the best practices from the automobile or airline industry possibly have to offer ECE? It turns out that some of the most powerful findings about the impact of positive relationships in the workplace have come out of research in these industries, showing that positive relationships matter in many sectors, such as business, health, education, and the military (Cameron & Spreitzer, 2012; Dutton & Ragins, 2007; Gittell, 2003; Gittell & Douglass, 2012).

A fascinating new body of research explores the role that relationships play in high-performing organizations across many diverse sectors and industries (Gittell, 2016). This research shows that positive relationships of mutual respect and shared power contribute to a wide range of positive outcomes, including quality; improvement and organizational learning; employee satisfaction, engagement, and retention; and client satisfaction and outcomes. This research points to the importance of relationships for cross-sector, cross-role professional collaboration, which is increasingly important in the transdisciplinary teams in which early educators work with family support, social work, mental health, early intervention, or other specialists. Organizations intentionally can promote and sustain these positive relationships by creating a relational system (Gittell & Douglass, 2012).

An important implication for early care and education is that designing organizations and systems with these relational structures can enable educators to be active agents of change and improvement (Douglass, 2014). This is a science that has yet to be applied in the ECE context, and this book explains why and how we must leverage this knowledge now to advance leadership, improvement, and innovation in the field.

A second relevant body of research comes from the science of improvement, a field that has figured prominently in the healthcare sector, contributing to breakthrough improvements in quality (Institute for Healthcare Improvement, 2003). Improvement science calls into question the typical approaches to quality improvement, ones used frequently in ECE and many other sectors, that often fail to achieve the desired results. As I describe in the first part of the book, insights from improvement science reveal that leading real and sustained change in organizations and systems is a highly relational team process in which groups of people involved at different levels of the work process must together co-create solutions that work in that local context. The co-creation process requires the engagement and leadership of early educators, as well as the formal leadership in ECE programs.

We do not need to reinvent the wheel to fix the persistent challenges we face. We have a history of women's leadership in our field and a long line of calls to develop and support diverse leadership from within (Goffin & Washington, 2007; Hinitz, 2013; Kagan & Bowman, 1997). We can benefit from the recent scientific advances in other fields and experiment with how best to apply those lessons to advance progress in our own field.

Leadership Pathways: Seeing the Possibilities of Leadership

By applying lessons on leadership and change from across our own and other disciplines, we can learn how to support and nurture a strong, diverse, and resilient workforce to lead change, improvement, and innovation in ECE. To do so, we must believe, and show the world, not only that early educators' leadership is possible, but that early educators possess unique knowledge and insights that are essential for understanding *how* to change and improve ECE.

For too long now, educators have been seen as the objects of change, rather than the architects and co-creators of change. This book reveals powerful stories of early educator leadership. Bringing these stories, and the possibility of early educator leadership, to the forefront is a transformative act in and of itself. It makes visible the leadership pathways of others and thus opens up new possibilities for leading. I have found that the idea of early educators as leaders and drivers of change is inconceivable to many both within and outside of our field, something I attribute to the deficit-oriented narrative about our field and our workforce, as well as persistent gender bias about leadership.

Part of the goal of professionalizing the field is not only to cultivate our own and our field's capacity to lead and drive change, but also to shift perceptions around our capacity to lead. We are bombarded with discouraging or negative messages about change and our workforce, and the messages in the headlines tend to focus on problems and deficits, rather than strengths. We rarely hear about the amazing and diverse leaders in ECE, or the ways we are resilient in change and persist in efforts to better serve children and families.

Before becoming a professor, I worked directly with children and families for almost 20 years. I taught children from birth to age 5, in family child care and center-based early learning programs, and I was a program director, owner, and quality improvement consultant. I thrived on the challenges of that work, as well as the incredible rewards of loving and teaching babies and young children, and partnering with their families, every single day. That work gave me a deep respect for the expertise, the leadership, and the caring professionalism of those who work most directly with children and their families. I saw firsthand the unique expertise that enabled these educators to understand better than anyone else what the real challenges and solutions are for transforming practices with children and families. As someone who now studies policy and practice in our field, I am struck by how rarely that expertise is recognized and tapped into as the driving force for improvement.

This book offers a framework for developing and elevating the leadership capabilities of early educators. I present data from several studies of leadership and change in ECE to illustrate the key components of this framework for nurturing the leadership ECE needs today and for the future. Embedding respectful relationships and educator leadership into professional development and quality improvement programming and systems is key.

A Leadership Development Ecosystem for ECE

Leadership is not a job title. It is a highly relational process of influencing change and improvement, and our field must develop an infrastructure that supports it. About a year ago, I was talking with graduates of the post-master's certificate leadership program that I direct. I learned that these early educators felt transformed in this leadership program and when they graduated were feeling energized and empowered to make change. Many had already had an impact: starting up a new preschool, implementing a change in practice at their center, testifying at a public hearing, or taking on a new leadership role in the profession. As one alumna said, "It's like an army of us has been created." But some were not sure how to take the next step to lead change, some were discouraged at the slow pace of change they were experiencing, and many lacked the resources needed to move forward and test the innovations they had designed.

I realized two things at that point. First, the leadership program had unleashed a powerful force for change within our field—the passion and insights of early educators, combined with their new knowledge and new mindsets. Second, it takes more than a leadership program to support and sustain leadership for change. We need to build a leadership and innovation ecosystem in our field to nurture and sustain early educator leaders throughout their careers and to more fully catalyze action for innovation and change in an ongoing way.

CONCLUSION

Developing leadership from within our field is an untapped lever for transforming early care and education, strengthening our workforce, and ensuring that all young children and their families thrive. Leadership and career pathways traditionally have been constructed as a sequence of linear steps into formal leadership positions in organizations or systems; however, as leadership increasingly is understood as a relational process of influencing change, which does not require a formal job title, the concept of a leadership pathway necessarily shifts. Rather than a predefined sequence of steps into formal leadership, a leadership pathway becomes a more emergent process that takes place in the context of one's work over time. The process of driving change requires ongoing resources and support. This support must become part of the environment in which early educators work, rather than only a one-time leadership development experience.

Here again, we can learn what this might look like from sectors that have well-developed leadership and innovation infrastructures. This book lays out the key components of an ECE leadership development ecosystem capable of nurturing leadership for change and innovation from within our field. The book concludes with a call to develop this leadership infrastructure, locally and at the systems level.

Part I

THEORETICAL AND RESEARCH FOUNDATION FOR LEADERSHIP AND CHANGE

CHAPTER 2

Rethinking Change in Early Care and Education

Our field is immersed in change, as we continually seek to improve the ways we serve young children and families, and support and strengthen our workforce and early childhood systems. The term *change* can conjure up a wide range of reactions, interpretations, and feelings. Change often is seen as difficult, even painful, something people tend to resist. Research tells us that efforts to make change often fail. Given all this, it is no surprise that training and quality improvement interventions frequently do not succeed in achieving their desired results. At the same time, many fields have become fascinated with innovation and new ideas. Some may see this trend as the latest fad, but others welcome this kind of thinking in our sector, which has long been overlooked by the methodologies and the resources in the innovation world.

This chapter presents current research and theory about change. This book focuses on change as improvement: changes we want, changes that help children and families, changes that help us thrive professionally and achieve better outcomes. Change here implies improvement, not just change for the sake of change. In this chapter I explore what makes change efforts succeed or fail, the science of improvement, and theories of organizational change and innovation. Relational organizational science, in particular, offers a rich body of theory and research evidence about change and improvement. Tapping into a multidisciplinary body of research and theory, this chapter offers a new way of thinking about how we might approach improvement and leadership for change in ECE settings and contexts.

CHANGE IN EARLY CARE AND EDUCATION

Forces both within and outside of our field are driving change. The common saying rings true in ECE: "The one constant in life is change." The science of early learning is advancing, and we are adopting new approaches to supporting the cognitive, language, physical, and social and emotional development of today's children. Our profession is pushing more strongly than ever before for the respect and fair compensation and working conditions we deserve. Research confirms the need to improve working conditions, retain diverse talent, and build supportive systems that enable early education professionals and programs to achieve and sustain high quality (Cameron, Mooney, & Moss, 2002; Douglass, 2011; Douglass & Klerman, 2012; Goldstein, 2007; Kagan & Kauerz, 2012; MacFarlane & Lewis, 2012; Wood & Bennett, 2000).

High-quality ECE is essential for children's healthy development and school readiness; however, too few children have access to the early learning experiences that matter most (Adams et al., 2007; Aikens, Bush, Gleason, Malone, & Tarullo, 2016; Hillemeier et al., 2013; Tout et al., 2016). Professional development and quality improvement are therefore increasingly important components of the ECE landscape today (Cameron et al., 2002; Douglass, 2014; Goldstein, 2007; Institute of Medicine & National Research Council, 2015; Kagan & Kauerz, 2012; MacFarlane & Lewis, 2012; Wood & Bennett, 2000). Local, state, and national efforts to strengthen access to high-quality ECE offer some successes, but the need to accelerate improvement and innovation in ECE is urgent.

Growing public attention to the importance of high-quality ECE has added to the pace of change. A great deal of emphasis has been placed on regulating quality from the top down through policy levers. This can increase external pressures for change in ECE programs. Many states are implementing new early learning standards, child assessment systems, coordinated professional development systems, and updated QRIS (Hyson & Whittaker, 2012; LeMoine, 2008; National Professional Development Center on Inclusion, 2008; Schaack et al., 2012; Stoney, Mitchell, & Warner, 2006; Tout, Metz, & Bartley, 2013). We do not yet know whether these policies will make a difference in improving quality, or how they might best be altered or adapted for better results (Connors, 2016; Douglass, Carter, Smith, & Killins, 2015; Tout et al., 2010).

We do know that sometimes early educators can find themselves overwhelmed or in conflict with the number, magnitude, pace, and sometimes even the purpose of the changes currently impacting the field, changes that are not always accompanied by adequate resources (Apple & McMullen, 2007; Douglass & Klerman, 2012; Goldstein, 2007; Satkowski, 2009). The change process, especially when driven by external pressures, is widely considered stressful (Cameron, 2008). In these times of rapid change, it is critical to know how to lead effectively and improve quality in ways that strengthen, rather than deplete, ourselves and the field.

CHALLENGES OF CHANGE

Why is change so difficult? Think about a change that has been made where you work that did not last. Why do you think it did not last? Some of us have experienced a change in which we were told what to change or how to change, but were unable to influence the changes that were being made, even if we knew better. Many of us have seen positive changes happen in a pilot or demonstration project, only to watch those good things disappear when funding dried up. Many educators have become accustomed to having change thrust upon them from some external source, driven by a new public policy or a regulatory agency. Sometimes the change involves implementing a new curriculum with fidelity, which means implementing it exactly as described in a publisher's manual. Sometimes the mandated changes do not come with sufficient resources to support implementing them effectively. Other times, the changes do not fit the individual needs of the children and families we serve. We may truly want to implement a change, but find that the process is overwhelming, and we are expected to change everything all at once. When we have made change, we may find it is difficult to sustain. A Head Start administrator shared this reflection on the challenges of trying to sustain change, explaining that "the pull back to the way we used to do things is so powerful."

What does all of this tell us about how to make changes that do stick? It certainly confirms the research evidence that change is a complex process. It points to important but sometimes invisible barriers to change. Understanding and addressing these can open up new possibilities for change and improvement. Next, we examine these key barriers to change in more depth.

UNDERSTANDING BARRIERS TO CHANGE

The degree of educators' readiness for change has drawn attention recently in the ECE research literature. The assumption here is that individuals who are open to change are more likely to adopt new practices; others are less likely to do so, but through additional support, some of them will. Research offers evidence to support this assumption (Peterson, 2013; Prochaska, 2008). Readiness to change is an important concept, but it also has limitations. The primary limitation is its typical focus on individuals and their resistance to change, at the expense of a more holistic understanding. The real barriers to change often have just as much or more to do with the workplace context than with any particular individual (Douglass, 2011). For example, if I am supposed to conduct a time-consuming quarterly comprehensive child assessment process for every child in my class and I do not have any paid planning time away from my responsibilities with the children, it probably will not matter how ready I am. I will need paid time away from the children, with access to technology, to complete and upload the assessments and to meet with parents and families to share information about their children's progress.

This focus on individuals is the dominant approach to quality improvement and professional development in ECE (Douglass & Klerman, 2012; Winton & McCollum, 2008). Training and individual coaching are common methods for improving teaching quality (Boller, Tarrant, & Schaack, 2014; Tout, Isner, & Zaslow, 2011). The rationale is that if we provide this training, teachers will learn new skills and apply them to their work. Many of our professional development systems are set up this way, so as to develop individuals' competencies. But it turns out that training is not enough.

Organizational Context: Culture and Structures

Individual-level approaches too often neglect important underlying relational, systemic, and organizational barriers to change (Connors, 2016; Douglass, 2011; Eaton, 2000; Hemmelgarn, Glisson, & Dukes, 2001; Winton & McCollum, 2008). Research across many sectors has found this to be the case. Training and coaching individuals alone is insufficient because it disregards the context in which they do their work (Ackerman, 2008; Douglass, Carter, et al., 2015; U.S. Department of Education, 2010). An organizational context may keep newly trained teachers from transferring what they have learned elsewhere into their current practice if it conflicts with the culture of the workplace (Eaton, 2000; Hemmelgarn et al., 2001). Teachers can learn new knowledge and skills through training and coaching, but research has shown that training can be wasted if they work in a setting where their newfound skills are not modeled, reinforced, or valued. Alternatively, we can design and improve the workplace context in ways that support and enhance educators' ability to change and improve (Douglass & Gittell, 2012; Gittell, 2016). The organizational context shapes what we do and how we do it. Here is an example that illustrates how that happens.

A few years ago, I conducted a study of child-care centers that were working to implement a family-engagement approach called Strengthening Families (Douglass, 2011; Douglass & Gittell, 2012; Douglass & Klerman, 2012). Over a 1-year period, I studied the family-engagement practices and organizational contexts in four large child-care centers that collectively served over 500 low-income children. I designed this as a multiple case study, in order to be able to compare each center with the others. This enabled me to better understand the factors that facilitated or interfered with improvement. I selected two centers that had high-quality family partnerships, and two that did not have high-quality family partnerships, enabling the cross-case comparisons. During that year, I conducted 20 hours of observations in each center, interviewed a total of 60 teachers and administrators, and examined center-written policies, records, and other documents.

This study looked at not only how teachers were trained, but also the workplace context and organizational culture and the ways that influenced teachers' adoption of new practices in their day-to-day work. Organizational culture—norms, values, assumptions, and shared meanings—is a strong influence on how people do their work. My study found that staff in centers where they did not feel respected or valued were less likely to develop positive and respectful relationships with parents (Douglass, 2011; Douglass & Klerman, 2012). An organizational culture of disrespect for staff was a barrier to family-centered practice. Linda, a teacher, explained to me: "If this center wants teachers to support families," the center "needs a 'strengthening staff' program. If you're falling apart, you can't be helping other people."

In contrast, in the centers where staff were treated with respect and supported, teachers extended that respect far more readily in their relationships with families. The relationships that staff experienced with other adults in the workplace carried over to their work with children and families. This discovery reveals the interconnectedness of workplace relationships and relationships with families and those we serve. The theory of parallel process explains how interactions among one set of individuals in an organization or a system can mirror, or parallel, interactions among another set of individuals (Parlakian, 2002).

This study found that a traditional bureaucratic organizational culture was a barrier to improving the quality of parent–teacher partnerships. In the bureaucratic organizations in the study, the organizational culture and policies in effect discouraged caring and responsive practices, and positioned the staff as experts with power over families. These organizations expected that all the rules and policies would be applied in the same manner with every family, regardless of circumstances or individual needs or culture. This policy interfered with the effort to adopt responsive and reciprocal partnerships with families. In contrast, programs that reflected a more relational organizational system fostered the opposite result: Leaders modeled shared power and expertise, and organizational processes and structures supported, valued, and rewarded caring and responsive relationships.

While this kind of organizational research is still new in early care and education, it is supported by a strong body of research conducted in other sectors, such as health. Research in health services has shown clearly that organizational factors, such as the organization's culture, influence the quality of client–professional relationships as well as client outcomes (Eaton, 2000; Gittell, 2002; Glisson & Hemmelgarn, 1998; Stone et al., 2002). This research shows that the relational organizational context is a critical learning environment that influences the extent to which professionals make changes to improve their practice. Organizational readiness is therefore an essential ingredient for successful quality improvement.

Yet changing the organizational context is rarely studied as a strategy for improving interventions and quality in human services or ECE (Yoo, Brooks, & Patti, 2007). Hemmelgarn et al. (2001) studied efforts to implement family-centered care in healthcare settings. They note that although most studies on this topic have focused on the training and characteristics of individuals as the primary determinant of family-centered care, in their study, the culture of the organization was the key factor. Similarly, in a study of nursing home care in California, Eaton (2000) found that improving the quality of care required more than training of staff: It required a major organizational paradigm shift to change the culture of care within the organization. This culture, reflected in its philosophy of care, was the central element shaping organizational processes and ultimately outcomes.

The U.S. Army also recognizes the important influence of team and organizational culture. A book based on its leadership manual explains:

> A climate or culture that saps morale robs the organization of one of its most precious assets. A culture that ensures high morale, on the other hand, promotes employee retention, commitment, and performance. People with high morale provide better services to customers, generate ideas for improvement, handle setbacks, encourage others, and more. With so much as stake, all organizations need to attend to their climate and culture with the same conscious intention as the Army does. (Hesselbein, Shinseki, & Cavanagh, 2004, p. 67)

The organizational context exerts a powerful influence on the ways we do our work. If we try to improve only individual skills and competencies without simultaneously focusing on the workplace context, we will not be successful when it comes to improvement: "You can't beat people into being compassionate; you can't mandate partnership. . . . Too often we find organizations with toxic cultures trying to help people be healthier—a sad irony" (Suchman, Sluyter, & Williamson, 2014, p. 42). The good news is that ECE has tools we can use to measure and improve organizational culture and climate, many of which have been developed by Paula Jorde Bloom (2005) and her colleagues at the McCormick Center for Early Childhood Leadership at National Louis University.

Organizational Structures: Breaking the Rules to Care

We can think of organizational systems as embodying three interrelated components: the *people* (staff, children, and families), *structures* within the organization (policies and procedures), and *processes* (organizational culture, "the way things are done" in the organization) (Bloom, 1991; Glisson, 2007). Organizational rules and policies are structures that can act as a barrier to change: A teacher can learn a set of new practices and be ready to change, but what if she tries to make these changes and finds herself in conflict with pertinent rules and policies?

Rules or policies may interfere with our ability to implement certain kinds of change. In my study of an initiative to improve parent–teacher partnerships, one teacher explained that she had to break the rules where she worked in order to be responsive to the needs of a family experiencing homelessness (Douglass & Klerman, 2012). This teacher found that one-size-fits-all policies in her program were a barrier to her adopting more responsive practices with the families she served. The sociology and organizational science literature is rich with similar findings about the constraints of rigid and bureaucratic structures and policies when it comes to relationship-based and caring work (Cancian, 2000; Fisher & Tronto, 1990; Gittell & Douglass, 2012; Lopez, 2006).

The teacher, Rosa, worked at a child-care center that served families in crisis. She had gone to a series of trainings about new ways to strengthen parent–teacher partnerships, particularly with families experiencing homelessness. She told me that to support the families she served, she often had to break the rules and she worried about being fired as a result. The center had a firm policy about morning arrival time for children. All children needed to be in their classroom's by 9 A.M. or they would not be allowed to attend that day. Three instances of tardiness were allowed, after which a family could risk being turned away, or even barred from the center, upon a late arrival. Rosa told me about a single-parent family that had become homeless and was moving from home to home among relatives. The mother had four children to send to school and child care each day, and with the frequent moves she had lost the option for her older children to ride the school bus. She was using public transportation each morning to get four children to three different schools, and she had prioritized getting the older kids to school on time. Rosa recognized the trade-offs this mother was making, and she wanted to be responsive to the needs of this family. She told the mother to drop off the child at whatever time she could, and promised not to mark the child late.

Rosa was afraid to speak up about this with her employer and her coworkers. She tried to stay under the radar, hoping she would not get fired. The rigid policies and supervisory climate in this center did not align with the day-to-day realities Rosa was facing. She felt herself caught between the organizational structures and culture and her desire to be responsive to the needs of her families.

Imagine, instead, if Rosa and the other teachers, parents, and administrators were working together to make improvements in family-engagement and support practices. What if they co-created new policies and practices to address the challenges posed by families in crisis and didn't leave teachers worrying that they might lose their jobs for doing what they believed was right? Without working together collaboratively as an organization, individuals often can't effectively improve what they do with children and families.

SYSTEMS THINKING

The scenario above points to the value of systems thinking as a solution to the difficulties described. Systems thinking helps us understand how change works—or doesn't—and how to get better outcomes in our efforts to make change (Bryk, Gomez, Grunow, & LeMahieu, 2015; Douglass, Carter, et al., 2015; Foster-Fishman & Behrens, 2007; Foster-Fishman, Nowell, & Yang, 2007).

A system is a whole that consists of two or more interdependent parts (Ackoff & Rovin, 2003). Its functioning depends on the interactions among its components. If we take it apart, it no longer functions. The individual components do not function either when they are disconnected from the system. With systems thinking, we appreciate that each part of a system interacts with and influences other parts. What matters is how the parts interact, not how each acts independently or on its own.

Systems thinker and scholar Russell Ackoff explains a system using the human body as an example. If we take the body apart, it no longer functions. And if we take out one part, for example, the eyes, they no longer see: They work only in the context of the system, not as an independent part. We can apply this same thinking to organizations. Most efforts to improve organizations "are directed at improving the parts but not at improving the whole. [As a result,] the parts don't form a system because they don't fit" (Ackoff, 2010). Changing one part of a system without paying attention to the other parts often leads to trouble. Systems thinking, instead, emphasizes the interrelationship among the parts and the whole, rather than the parts seen in isolation (Hargreaves, 2010).

Systems thinking is hardly new. The field of early childhood education has long been familiar with it in regard to children's development. Bronfenbrenner's ecological systems theory has helped us understand how children develop in the context of the multiple environments and relationships around them. Children do not grow and learn in isolation, or only as a result of their parental or educational experiences. They are influenced by, and they actively influence, the environments and relationships closest to them, as well as those more distally located. This is why parent–teacher partnerships are so important in education: Teachers and families and children influence one another in powerful and sometimes unpredictable or unexpected ways.

When it comes to change and improvement, systems work in much the same way. Teachers do not work in isolation; rather, they work in multiple contexts, all of which exert influences to varying degrees. When teachers try to change, they are influenced by the environments in which they operate. These environmental factors include the individual, teaching team, classroom, organization, community, and state contexts. When they try to make changes, teachers influence those environments in turn. Their practices are shaped by the interactions among their own individual context, their classrooms, the workplace, the community, and more distal political, economic, cultural, and social contexts.

When quality improvement and change efforts intervene at only the individual level, they are less likely to have a lasting impact. For example, an infant teacher once told me that she was trying to improve the quality of her partnership with parents. She wanted to implement a practice of greeting and talking informally with each parent when the parents dropped their babies off in the morning. But to do this, she needed to shift the staffing pattern in her classroom to enable her to have time to engage directly with parents while the babies were cared for by another member of her teaching team. She saw how her practice was embedded within the larger systems and structures of the workplace. She was able to work effectively with the other staff and administrators to find a creative way to shift the staffing patterns to support these new parent–teacher partnership practices, while still adhering to budgetary and licensing realities.

The teachers' stories shared here illustrate the interconnections between teachers' practices and their workplace (and community) contexts. These interconnections have been documented in research from other sectors and are beginning to become a focus of emerging research in ECE (Connors, 2016; Derrick-Mills, Sandstrom, Pettijohn, Fyffe, & Koulish, 2014; Douglass, 2011; Douglass & Gittell, 2012; French & Wagner, 2010). Making change is a collaborative or team process, not just an individual endeavor. Making change is about seeing the whole and attending to the interconnections among the parts. Making change is about relationships, because people and their relationships are the interconnecting, interacting, and dynamic lifeblood of ECE systems. Because of this, we need to focus not just on individuals, or individual competencies, when it comes to quality improvement. Professional development needs to occur in the context of the workplace. Similarly, leadership development must occur in the context of leaders' work: We should not just send leaders away for professional development, but instead bring the leadership development into the contexts where they work (Raelin, 2011).

THE SCIENCE OF RELATIONAL COORDINATION

A growing body of research on relational organizational systems offers key insights that can help us understand what kinds of relationships facilitate effective change. Relationships are a core element of any human system. Early educators understand the power of relationships better than just about anyone else. Positive nurturing relationships are the basis for our work with babies and children, and the foundation for their learning. But ECE has largely failed to translate this attention to relationships into the adult realm in the workplace. And few efforts to improve quality include a focus on strengthening the workplace climate, although the research in this chapter highlights the influence of a positive workplace environment on quality and improvement.

Since the late 1990s, the organizational science literature has developed a strong theoretical and research base about positive relationships at work. The relational organizational science literature offers key insights for ECE. This body of research illuminates the essential role relationships play in high-performing organizations and systems in diverse sectors and industries (Gittell, 2016; Golden-Biddle & Mao, 2012; Suchman et al., 2014). This research shows that relationships of mutual respect and shared power are vital in helping organizations achieve positive outcomes, such as service quality; improvement and organizational learning; employee satisfaction, engagement, and retention; and client satisfaction and outcomes (Gittell, Seidner, & Wimbush, 2010). We saw this in action in Linda's observation that her organization needed to strengthen staff relationships in order to strengthen parent–teacher relationships. Research shows that the relational quality of the workplace influences virtually every aspect of organizational performance (Suchman et al., 2014). Most important for change efforts, these positive relationships can enable organizational members to respond in resilient ways to internal and external pressures for change (Gittell, 2008).

Relational coordination theory explains how this works (Gittell, 2002, 2003; Gittell & Douglass, 2012). A relational organizational system has two main parts: the relationships among people, including the ways they interact and communicate, and organizational structures, such as policies and protocols. These two parts of the relational organizational system are not separate: They are mutually reinforcing. The structures support, enable, and sustain the positive relationships. Relational coordination theory, and the evidence that supports it, confirms that positive relationships at work matter: They help us do our work better (Dutton & Ragins, 2007; Gittell, 2016). High-quality relationships among the people working in different roles across an organization are the most important ingredient for achieving desired outcomes.

What kinds of relationships matter? Research shows that positive relationships at work have the following characteristics: mutual respect, shared goals, and shared knowledge. Mutual respect refers to people's respect for one another, regardless of their role or status within the organization. Shared goals refer to staff throughout a team or organization having a shared goal about the work they do collectively. Shared knowledge refers to shared understanding about how one's work or role interrelates with the work of others and in the organization as a whole. This is called relational coordination, when we respect and understand the work of others and the ways in which everyone's roles contribute to the organization (Gittell, 2016). These high-quality relationships reinforce, and are reinforced by, high-quality communication, defined as being frequent, timely, accurate, and focused on problem solving rather than on blaming.

Figure 2.1. Relational Map

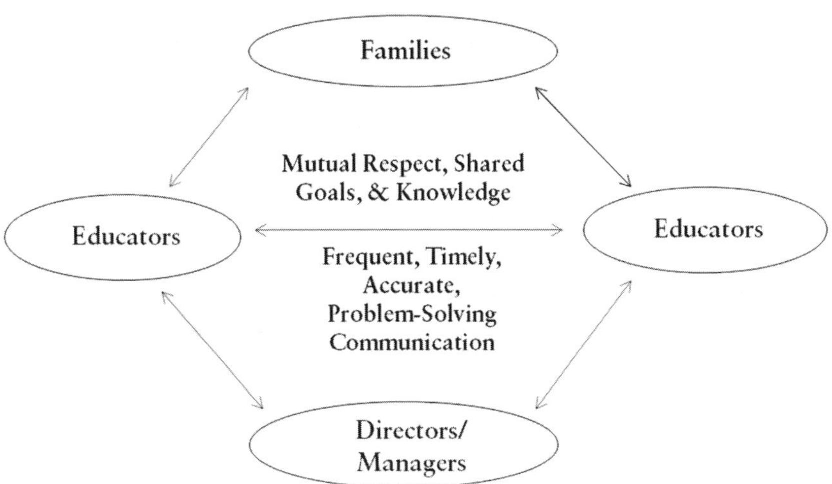

Take a look at this map of relationships, often referred to as a relational map, in one ECE program (see Figure 2.1). Research shows that it is easier to make change and improvement when these relationships are strong.

The map shows one way of visualizing relationships within an organization. Everyone's work is focused on the same thing: helping the children at the center to succeed. To provide the best care for the children, the relationships between and among these groups of people must be strong. When these ties—the lines connecting groups—are strong, when mutual respect is strong, it is easier to make change and improvement, and to deliver child- and family-centered practice. Respect for the expertise of people in each of the roles in the organization is essential. For example, the expertise of teachers and families is recognized and valued. This respect enables leadership to emerge at all levels. And this leadership is the driving force for change—what most often makes the difference between a successful change effort and one that fails.

Now we turn to the structures part of relational coordination. Relational coordination research identifies specific organizational structures that can help enable, develop, and sustain these positive relationships (Douglass, 2011; Gittell, 2016). If we leave these relationships up to chance, if it's just that you and I have a good relationship because we happen to like each other, then we don't embed these relationships throughout our whole organization in sustainable ways. This is why we need the structures.

This may seem counterintuitive. At first, we might assume that structures would get in the way of relationships. And it is sometimes true: That is exactly what happens in bureaucratic organizations. Certain kinds of

Imagine creating a relational map like this where you work:

- Where do you find these respectful relationships and good communication happening between the different roles or teams where you work?
- How do those positive relationships and effective communication enhance your ability to do good work and make improvements?
- Can you find places where those relationships and that communication can be stronger?
- What is one step you can take to improve and strengthen those relationships?

An exercise like this can help make these relationships more visible, with their strengths and gaps, so you can see where to focus your energies.

structures—like the rigid rules and policies discussed above—can keep responsive and caring practices from happening. In that situation, if people want to be responsive and flexible in serving families, they may decide they have to break the rules, as Rosa did. Rigid structures can interfere with people's ability to make changes to serve children and families well (Douglass, 2011). Thus, it is not just any structures that are needed. We need special kind of structures, relational structures, to support high-quality, family-centered practice.

You might be wondering what an example of a relational structure would be (see Figure 2.2).

Think about orientation and staff training protocols. Does your staff orientation policy address teaching team relationships and communication? Do you have formal procedures or protocols for communication among and between different teams or roles in your organization? These are examples of relational structures. Relational structures influence relationships in ways that support and enhance their quality and sustainability.

Organizations with these positive relationships get better outcomes. They are more effective when it comes to change and improvement, they are more resilient, the people who work there are more satisfied, and turnover occurs less often (Gittell, 2016). Designing organizations and systems with these relational structures can enable educators to be agents of change and improvement (Douglass, 2014). When, instead, organizations overlook the influence of relationships and mutual respect, and fail to organize in ways that enhance relationships, they are far less likely to achieve these desired outcomes. So these relationships are not merely a nice thing to have; they are the foundation for learning to improve the kinds of highly complex and relational work we do.

Figure 2.2. Designing Relational Structures

Relational Structures	Example
Hiring for relational competencies	Specific criteria for relational competencies (working effectively with adults, including demonstrated track record of respectful relations at work with colleagues, supervisors, and families) are included in job descriptions, job postings, and interview and hiring processes.
Inclusive team meetings	Regular cross-role meetings bring together staff and administrators from different classrooms and offices to work collaboratively on common areas for improvement and to gain deeper understanding of the ways in which each person's work relates to the work of others.
Flexible protocols	Protocols are established to provide a clear and coordinated way for staff to be responsive, flexible, and supportive in their partnerships with families.
Rewards for relational competencies	Performance evaluation for teachers, administrators, and other staff includes assessment of relational practices and communication with other adults, not just with children.
Training for relational competencies	Training and professional development include a focus on effective teamwork, communication, and problem solving among adults and with families.

How can you make an organization more relational? You can do this in two ways: You can intervene to change the structures—the policies and routines—in the organization, and you can intervene directly to strengthen relationships. To build or improve a relational organization, you need to do both. So where do you start? Evidence is emerging that you are unlikely to make progress without some degree of mutual respect (Gittell, 2016). Therefore, strengthening mutual respect for expertise and leadership at all levels is a good place to start. This book offers many ideas and concrete strategies for increasing respect for and among early educators.

THE SCIENCE OF IMPROVEMENT

A related and complementary body of research comes from improvement science, a field that has figured prominently in the healthcare sector, contributing to breakthrough improvements in quality (Institute for Healthcare Improvement, 2003). Improvement science incorporates systems thinking and offers evidence-based methodologies for making effective and lasting change (Bryk et al., 2015; Deming, 1986; Langley et al., 2009). It offers an alternative to the dominant approaches to quality improvement, still used frequently in ECE and many other sectors, which often fail to achieve the desired results. Implementation science is a related but different field that has been the focus of some of the ECE research literature (Halle, Metz, & Martinez-Beck, 2013). Improvement science studies the ways in which, and the extent to which, interventions are implemented as intended. Improvement science places a specific focus on improvement and on learning about how to make change in ways that result in improvement (Bryk et al., 2015).

Insights from improvement science reveal that leading real and sustained change in organizations and systems is a highly relational, team process in which groups of people who work at different levels come together to co-create solutions that work in their local context. This sounds very much like the key insights from relational organizational science and systems thinking. The engagement and leadership of people from all levels of an organization are important when it comes to making effective and lasting change.

One significant contribution from the field of improvement science is the Breakthrough Series Collaborative methodology, developed by the Institute for Healthcare Improvement in 2003. Its purpose is to close the gap between what we know to be good practice and what we actually do in our work. It helps us make changes that enhance the outcomes we want to achieve. It is an evidence-based, structured process that typically takes place over a year. Under the guidance of an individual called an improvement advisor, teams of staff from multiple organizations are engaged in cycles of collaborative learning and improvement. Teams consist of both the organization's formal leadership and those working on the front lines. The method focuses on the use of data to determine the best strategies to achieve targeted outcomes in the local context, and then to promote the spread and sustainability of these improvements.

When this methodology is successfully implemented, the changes made in organizations are sustainable (Backer, Kiser, Gilham, & Smith, 2015; Bitton et al., 2014; Boushon, Provost, Gagnon, & Carver, 2006; Ebert, Amaya-Jackson, Markiewicz, Kisiel, & Fairbank, 2012). The experience of making change that works and is sustained, is empowering and energizing, and can fuel continued improvement, as reflected by a nurse from Tennessee: "Once you start this, you can't stop it. People want to keep on changing things, improving things. After every success, they just keep asking, 'What can we do next?'" (Institute for Healthcare Improvement, 2003, p. 12).

The Breakthrough Series Collaborative methodology leverages the power of forming organizational cross-role teams that bring complementary expertise, insights, and authority to determine what to change and how best to change it. It works by strengthening leadership at all levels and recognizes that professional development and quality improvement need to be embedded in the contexts in which people work. For 2 decades, it has been widely used in healthcare settings in the United States and around the world. More recently, the method was adapted for the child welfare sector (Agosti, Conradi, Halladay Goldman, & Langan, 2013). Now it is being explored and tested in education and ECE settings (Arbour et al., 2016; Bryk et al., 2015; Douglass, 2016b; Office of Planning, Research and Evaluation, 2017).

Most ECE quality improvement approaches have focused on top-down, externally driven, accountability-focused methods for improvement (Douglass, 2014; Goldstein, 2007; Kagan & Kauerz, 2012). The Breakthrough Series Collaborative methodology for change offers an alternative way to think about and make change. Chapter 7 describes how the methodology was tested in the ECE sector to promote trauma-informed practices in urban early education settings in one city.

INNOVATION

What is innovation, and how can it contribute to our thinking about change and improvement? When people confront challenges or persistent problems in their work, they sometimes, individually or collectively, generate solutions or new practices or service delivery models. This likely happens all the time, including in the ECE sector, but we don't often hear about it or call it innovation. Innovation is about having a vision for doing things better, being willing to think creatively "outside the box," and being passionate about change and inspiring others (Smith & Petersen, 2006).

Thinking in innovative ways can expand or redefine our ideas about what is possible. Innovation is particularly important when organizations or systems are experiencing one or more of the following conditions: changing expectations, changing policy or economic landscape, the acquisition of new knowledge, or a change in access to resources such as funding. Do any of these conditions influence your work? I would suspect that for many, the answer is yes. The introduction of QRIS often changed expectations for what early educators and programs should be doing. Similarly, learning new knowledge about how best to promote children's development can shift our own expectations about our practice. Innovation is one way we, individually and collectively, can make changes to solve our problems or meet a new or unmet need.

The ECE field can learn from the innovation sector about how to create organizational cultures and systems that nurture, rather than stifle, innovation. Innovation thrives in certain kinds of environments. For example, a workplace culture of experimentation and creativity can enable innovation. Regular opportunities for adults to talk and examine data together can result in new ideas and solutions. Organizations and teams can foster innovation when people feel safe voicing a new or different way of thinking about a problem and/or its solution.

However, many education systems and organizations do not cultivate these kinds of environments: In many ECE settings, adults do not have regular opportunities to meet, reflect on data, and creatively experiment with new ideas and solutions. Additionally, "the focus on compliance and implementation of programs in much of today's professional development does not inspire teachers to be creative, nor does it foster a culture of innovation. . . . We've created conditions in which creative and innovative educators must 'break the rules' to try new ideas to promote student learning" (Couros, 2015, p. 5). Creativity is at the heart of both innovation and learning. We regularly observe, cultivate, and find joy in the boundless creativity of young children, and we need to extend that to ourselves and our field.

Both the innovation sector and the field of improvement science talk about how we can effectively cultivate creative problem solving and generate innovative solutions. For example, human-centered design methods offer a set of tools and protocols for drawing on the expertise of the people closest to a problem to inform transformative solutions. Rather than just looking to "outside" experts to create solutions, human-centered design goes directly to the "inside" experts—the users, customers, and, in our field, the children, families, owners, and staff in ECE programs. As the Stanford University design school explains, "This approach sets aside the idea that there is an off-the-shelf solution to solving the challenges we face. To address these challenges, it is essential to understand the needs of those who experience the problem, and co-design and test solutions in real-world settings" (static1.squarespace.com/static/57c6b79629687fde090a0fdd/t/58890239db29d6cc6c3338f7/1485374014340/METHODCARDS-v3-slim.pdf). These insights are yet another confirmation that we have many more options than we currently draw upon for how we make change in our field. The improvement and innovation research suggests we may be far more effective when we employ these more collaborative, creative, user-centric approaches (George, 2007; Kilo, 1998; Langley et al., 2009; Senge, 2006).

Innovation is important for another reason, too. The children of today will be the innovators of the future, and their future jobs will likely require creativity and an innovative mindset. If we want to cultivate children's imagination and creativity, we need to create the conditions that nurture those same qualities in our ECE programs and the workforce. Research shows that children's learning can be enhanced when the learning environment and the educators in that environment demonstrate and model creativity, curiosity, and imagination in their everyday routines and interactions (Kunnari & Ilomäki, 2016; Stone-MacDonald, Wendell, Douglass, & Love, 2015).

The early care and education sector may be especially and uniquely conducive to innovation. ECE is made up largely of small businesses, in contrast to the K–12 sector, which operates primarily as a single unified system. ECE is subject to far fewer bureaucratic constraints than the K–12 education sector, making it an exceptionally innovation-friendly space. This can enable enormous variation and experimentation, conditions that have been so difficult to achieve in the K–12 sector yet are ideal for innovation. We can see this as a strength, if we recognize the potential it offers to allow for innovation, variation, and experimentation. One way to improve the ECE system is to build supportive systems that recognize and capitalize on the small-business and mixed-delivery-system model in this sector. When we try to fix problems within ECE with solutions that work in the K–12 sector, we should consider whether those solutions are a smart fit for such a different sector with a unique set of strengths and possibilities.

CONCLUSION

Change is a defining feature of early care and education, just as it is in so many other sectors and in our world. Yet, as this chapter has highlighted, making change can be exceedingly difficult under current conditions. Disempowering and disrespecting front-line staff, like teachers, is a barrier to change. Failing to provide adequate support for implementing new practices is a barrier to change, as is pushing mandated changes down on early childhood programs in prescriptive ways. Working in an organization with low morale or an organizational culture of disrespect can work against change and improvement. We know from systems theory and relational science that we cannot expect results when we touch only one part of the whole. We cannot continue to expect and hope for change to happen under conditions that we know are most unlikely to result in improvement.

We need to expand the ways in which we think about and make change, so that we can be more effective in fulfilling our vision. The research on relational systems, improvement, and innovation contributes key insights that point to new directions for how we can make change in our field.

Key Insights for Making Change in Our Field

- The organizational context is a powerful influence on teachers' practices and capacity to improve.
- Positive relationships at work matter, especially when it comes to making change and improvement.
- Organizations can create environments that enable and support positive relationships and mutual respect, and cultivate the creativity that drives innovation.
- These relational organizational systems can elevate the leadership of educators as change agents and result in improved outcomes for change.

Designing relational systems can enable educators to be active agents of change, improvement, and innovation. The research presented in this chapter affirms that any effort to effect change must tap into and elevate that expertise. The following chapter delves into the question of what kind of leadership is needed to drive positive change. The chapter offers a multidisciplinary, cross-sector perspective on what kind of leadership is needed and how to cultivate and strengthen it.

CHAPTER 3

Rethinking Leadership in Early Care and Education

For just a minute, imagine one thing you most want to change in order to improve your work or your organization's capacity to serve children and families. Most of us have something we would like to see changed. When we do, we are usually more than ready for change. When we want to change something, we often have intimate knowledge and expertise about the problem, and because of that, we have keen insights into the possible solutions. We assume some level of ownership for the change, and we may even lead the effort to do something about it. We can learn the most about change from the things we care most about changing.

The importance of being invested and engaged when it comes to change is a key insight, and this is confirmed in research across disciplines. At the heart of many unsuccessful change efforts is the failure to engage the expertise and the leadership of people at all levels of the organization. The research reviewed in the previous chapter emphasizes that change must include the expertise and leadership of those most directly involved in the work. Leadership from all levels and roles within organizations is a key ingredient for successful and lasting change. Leadership and change go hand in hand. To strengthen our field and improve what we do with children and families, we must build leadership capacity.

People tend to think of leadership as a formal position with a job title. This book adopts a broader and more inclusive definition: It defines leadership as a process of influencing change to achieve a positive outcome to improve early care and education. Leaders are people who can improve children's and families' lives. Leadership is something we do, not a job title or person.

This kind of leadership drives success across sectors, from business, the military, and health, to the public sector. Research in the K–12 education and social innovation sectors proves that educator leadership can dramatically improve children's learning. Educator leadership has the potential to reap similarly dramatic benefits in the ECE sector. No one is better suited to lead change than those most involved in the work processes we seek to improve.

Throughout this book, I argue that immense untapped potential for improvement lies within the early care and education workforce. By supporting and strengthening this leadership, we uncover the key to transformative change that will benefit the millions of young children and families we serve. This chapter explores the current research on relational, collaborative, and entrepreneurial forms of leadership, and examines how cultivating this inclusive notion of leadership contributes to change and improvement.

THE CHALLENGE AND THE OPPORTUNITY: DEVELOPING LEADERSHIP FOR CHANGE IN ECE

Advancing quality and professionalizing ECE will require a strong and diverse cadre of leaders at all levels, capable of driving continuous improvement and facilitating transformative change and innovation. Yet the early care and education field faces a leadership development gap (Goffin, 2013). ECE lacks clearly defined and articulated leadership development opportunities and pathways. Experienced early educators lack opportunities to grow throughout their careers and develop the skills they need in order to lead (Ramgopal et al., 2009; Taba et al., 1999). Hitting this kind of professional plateau can leave teachers feeling burned out, stymied, and losing passion for their field. It can result in a loss of talent from the field, just when it is most needed. These striking gaps are mirrored in the ECE research literature, which as yet has just scratched the surface on leadership (Bloom & Sheerer, 1992; Muijs, Aubrey, Harris, & Briggs, 2004; Wise & Wright, 2012).

Almost no public or private investments target leadership development in a systematic way in the birth-to-5 ECE sector, in striking contrast to investments in leadership development in other sectors. Little attention has been paid to building systems for developing and supporting the leadership of early educators to drive improvement (Goffin, 2013; Kagan & Bowman, 1997). Unlike other fields, such as healthcare, ECE lacks a unified leadership infrastructure (Goffin & Janke, 2013). In the healthcare sector, for example, leadership from within the field has long been identified as a key driver of improvement (Berwick, 1994). Quality improvement interventions have been designed to tap into and cultivate this leadership (Institute for Healthcare Improvement, 2003).

This ECE leadership development gap is not new. In the mid-1990s, Kagan and Bowman (1997) highlighted the absence of leadership development capacity in the field: "Leadership is a preferred domain for investment in most institutions—one that yields long-term, cost-efficient rewards. Early Care and Education should not be an exception to this reality" (p. 5). With today's renewed attention to the ECE workforce, it is critical to build up the leadership development infrastructure. Much attention to ECE workforce development focuses on teacher competencies and credentials at the entry level. While this is essential, we do not yet have a comparable focus on how to support and retain experienced early educators. Turnover is recognized as a central challenge, and yet we have not built professional development systems that might nurture, elevate, and retain the expertise of experienced educators.

Pockets of promising ECE leadership development activity and innovation can be found across the country, primarily focused on leadership and management training for program administrators (Bloom & Bella, 2005; Carr, Johnson, & Corkwell, 2009; Goffin & Janke, 2013; Whitebook, Kipnis, Sakai, & Austin, 2012; Woodrow & Busch, 2008). Goffin and Janke, in particular, examined and categorized 55 independent ECE leadership development programs across the United States. They compiled and analyzed their findings in a compendium that identifies the existing models for leadership development programming. This compendium provides critical data about the current state of leadership development that can inform thinking about how to build a more systemic approach to developing leadership for change.

IMPACT OF ECE LEADERSHIP DEVELOPMENT

The scale and diversity of the ECE workforce and its potential leadership impact are immense. Our sector employs more educators than the K–12 education system in the United States. Early educators constitute 30% of the entire instructional workforce from early childhood to postsecondary education (National Research Council, 2012). Early educators serving children from birth to 5 years old are the most racially, ethnically, and linguistically diverse sector of the education workforce from birth to postsecondary school. However, compensation, professional recognition, and professional development fall short of what this sector needs. The birth-to-5 education workforce is the lowest-paid sector of the entire education workforce. Early educator salaries are so low that almost half rely on public assistance to make ends meet (Whitebook, 1999; Whitebook, Phillips, & Howes, 2014; Whitebook & Sakai, 2003). When it comes to leadership jobs, ECE directors and administrators earn noticeably less than their counterparts in the public schools, and they have less access to professional development supports (Wise & Wright, 2012). The median salary of a high school principal in 2012 was $87,760, while the median salary of a preschool director was barely half that much, at $43,950 (Bureau of Labor Statistics, 2014). Men, despite their low numbers in the ECE workforce overall, are overrepresented in ECE leadership. A 2012 study of the ECE workforce in California (Whitebook et al.) found that although 8% of participants identified as male, 16% of center directors were male. Even in this predominantly female profession, a focus on supporting women's leadership is important. Equally important is supporting racial and linguistic diversity in leadership, which requires that leadership development programs and systems are fully inclusive of the rich diversity within our workforce.

Strong leadership within the field has the potential to raise the status of the ECE workforce and drive quality improvement. Early educator leadership can act as a catalyzing force to establish equitable compensation. More than 2 million strong, early educators equip and inspire the next generation to do great things. Each week, more than 10 million children ages 0–5 are cared for by early educators (Child Care in America, 2016). When we build talent from within this workforce, we tap this passion, insight, and leadership in order to revolutionize educational outcomes. Leadership development truly is the next frontier in professionalizing our field.

UNDERSTANDING THE LEADERSHIP DEVELOPMENT GAP

There is a gap and an opportunity here. How do we take advantage of this opportunity to expand leadership development in ECE? A foundation for building a leadership development system in our field is an inclusive, purpose-driven, and relational definition of leadership. Several studies have noted a historical tension or misalignment between dominant notions of leadership and the kind of leadership that is needed or practiced in ECE (Grieshaber, 2001; Morgan, 1997). We need to think about leadership in ways that resonate within our field, so that leadership is a path for many, not just a few.

Definitions of Leadership

Many of the educators I teach have never thought of themselves as leaders. They have had to redefine what leadership is and what it means for them to begin to see the leadership within. I teach a course on leadership, and in the first session I ask educators to think about what comes to mind when they hear the word *leader* or *leadership*. They come up with images of heroic figures, powerful people in high-level positions, and people who are assertive, decisive, and commanding. But these educators almost never associate themselves with those traits; they almost never identify themselves as leaders.

Leadership research historically has focused on individuals in formal positions of power who possess traits such as assertiveness, decisiveness, control, and domination, often reflecting traditionally masculine identities (Fletcher, 2004). Much of existing leadership theory was developed in the industrial age, and as a result it emphasized the goals of achieving control, stability, and efficiency in producing goods and products (Uhl-Bien, Marion, & McKelvey, 2007). This notion of leadership has been critiqued as incompatible or misaligned with the predominantly female ECE workforce

(Douglass & Gittell, 2012; Henderson-Kelly & Pamphilon, 2000; Rodd, 1998; Wise & Wright, 2012). Rodd (1998) refers to an aversion to leadership in ECE and suggests the need to redefine leadership so it better aligns with the field. Goffin (2013) writes about some of the mindsets in ECE that can constrain our leadership. One of these mindsets is the tendency to depend on others to advance our field's merit. She describes how public policy and government agencies have played an oversized role in driving the changes in our field. Referring to our field's own advocacy agenda, she argues that "limiting internal change to what the general public and policymakers will support promotes dependence on others" (p. 19).

Wise and Wright (2012) and Rodd (1998) argue that a more relational and collaborative form of leadership is a better fit for ECE and its highly relational and complex work. Sullivan (2009) and Heikka and Waniganayake (2011) extend this line of thinking to advocate for utilizing a distributed approach to leadership in early childhood centers; in this approach, everyone in a given organization has at least one leadership opportunity and responsibility, and making mistakes is accepted and encouraged. Wise and Wright (2012) call for expanding the definition of leadership within the ECE field to be inclusive of the ways in which women's experiences as leaders are developed and constructed.

These concerns with traditional notions of leadership are shared by other sectors, even the business world. Research has found that traditional leadership often is not a good fit for modern organizations and businesses. For example, in an article on Danish leaders who were implementing change in 26 different organizations, Christiansen and Higgs (2010) report that "leader centric behaviors" had an adverse impact on change implementation (p. 1). As a result, relational forms of leadership have begun to attract broad interest because they align better with the environments of contemporary organizations and businesses.

Relational Leadership

Relational leadership scholars define leadership differently—as a process of influencing change to achieve a shared goal by turning knowledge and ideas into action to solve problems. This kind of leadership is inherently action-oriented. It is leadership that is open to all. Its definition is rooted in the understanding that leadership can be exercised by individuals and groups at all levels, regardless of formal titles or roles (Fletcher, 2004; Gittell & Douglass, 2012). Relational leadership is associated with high-performing organizations across many sectors (Gittell, 2016). In helping professions such as nursing, engaging in authentic leadership has been associated with lower levels of emotional exhaustion and cynicism and improved employee well-being (Hadley, 2014; Laschinger, Wong, & Grau, 2013). Leadership has been found to foster employee creativity, leading to increased organizational effectiveness (Rego, Sousa, Marques, & Cunha, 2012).

Leadership increasingly is recognized as a collaborative and relational process for accomplishing positive change (Fletcher, 2004; Komives, Lucas, & McMahon, 2007; Ospina & Foldy, 2010; Uhl-Bien & Ospina, 2012). Relational forms of leadership carry many different labels (relational, collective, collaborative, distributed, and shared), but they all share a common view that leadership is a process that is inherently relational and exercised at multiple levels, often by both formal and informal leaders (Ancona & Bresman, 2007; Douglass & Gittell, 2012; Fletcher, 1999). Gittell and Douglass (2012) have theorized that relational leadership is a process of co-creation, in which the expertise held by each individual contributes to a more holistic perspective, which better informs decisions, actions, or thinking:

> Relational leadership owes much to the concepts of distributed and shared leadership. However, relational leadership does more than draw upon expertise and leadership from participants throughout the organization. It is a process of reciprocal interrelating through which the expertise held by different participants interpenetrates, creating a more holistic perspective that is integrative rather than additive. Relational leadership thus requires the ability to facilitate the interpenetration of expertise among others such that their expertise is not simply added up but, rather, each participant is influenced by the other to achieve a more integrated understanding of the situation. (p. 720)

It may come as a surprise that the U.S. Army has developed a distributed, relational, and collaborative leadership model:

> No one is only a leader; each person in an organization is also a follower and a part of a team. In fact, the old distinction between leaders and followers has blurred; complex twenty-first-century organizations require individuals to move seamlessly from one role to another in an organization, from leadership to "followership" and back again. (Hesselbein et al., 2004, p. 18)

Like other forms of relational leadership, the Army's leadership model is reciprocal, focused on including the expertise of many and on the capacity of individuals at all levels to enter into and out of leadership in a fluid manner. Here again, leadership is something people do, not a title. Relational leadership is about creating connections and influencing positive change. The parallel between this understanding of leadership and the core work of early educators is striking. Who could be more skilled at creating connections and promoting positive development than early educators? It is the heart of what we do.

Entrepreneurial Leadership

Entrepreneurial leadership is another form of leadership that holds great promise for transforming quality and retaining talented, experienced, and diverse early educators. Although entrepreneurial leadership has received little mention in the ECE context, I argue that it aligns strongly with our field.

What is entrepreneurial leadership? Entrepreneurs seek out new, better, and more adaptive solutions to complex problems. They are a kind of innovator who strives for transformative change (Smith & Petersen, 2006). The hallmark of entrepreneurial leadership is the relentless pursuit of better ways to do things (Leonard, 2013). Traditional managerial leadership works fine when it comes to solving technical problems for which a solution is readily available, such as how to accurately and efficiently track parents' fee payments. Adaptive challenges, in contrast, are problems for which an existing or predefined solution is unavailable. These kinds of challenges require the innovative thinking that is the hallmark of entrepreneurial leadership. Entrepreneurship traditionally has been associated only with the business sector; however, a growing focus on educational and social entrepreneurs shines a light on the ways educators or other professionals can tap into their insights, passion, and knowledge to create new solutions and improve outcomes (Hess, 2006; Leonard, 2013; Smith & Petersen, 2006). Sometimes people distinguish between entrepreneurs and "intrapreneurs." In the strict definition, entrepreneurs are outsiders who make change and innovate from the outside of a sector or an organization. "Intrapreneurs" are the innovators who work from within the system or organization (Smith & Petersen, 2006). Smith and Petersen argue that in entrenched bureaucratic systems, such as K–12 education, organizations cannot or will not "disrupt" themselves, and so this requires outsiders to be the drivers of transformative change. To avoid unnecessary jargon, I have chosen to use the general term *entrepreneurial leadership* to refer to the leadership of those within, as well as outside of, ECE organizations or systems. The early care and education sector is quite different from the K–12 context, and it cannot easily be characterized as an entrenched bureaucratic system. Moreover, our field often has been told what to do by outsiders, and it is high time we cultivated strong, entrepreneurial leadership from within our ranks to lead improvement and innovation.

Entrepreneurial leadership is probably the least recognized form of leadership in ECE. Many of the major books on ECE leadership published over the years have examined managerial, advocacy, conceptual, instructional, or pedagogical leadership, and the kinds of skills, competencies, and dispositions each requires. Similar to other traditional and dominant notions of leadership, entrepreneurial leadership carries masculine identities (Calás,

Smircich, & Bourne, 2009). In fact, even in the business realm, women often do not think of themselves as innovators or entrepreneurs (Muntean & Özkazanç-Pan, 2016). Social entrepreneurship is entrepreneurship in social and educational contexts that seeks to drive social change or educational innovation. Muntean and Özkazanç-Pan (2016), in their feminist analysis of social entrepreneurship, explain that the "social" in social entrepreneurship, and its focus on social change, may evoke more feminine or inclusive thinking. Yet they note that even "the social entrepreneur is described as heroic, ambitious, courageous, strong and enterprising—a distinctly masculine description" (pp. 222–223).

While entrepreneurial leadership may be less familiar to our field, it is an important realm of leadership for ECE right now. Entrepreneurial leaders in ECE create and grow ECE businesses and turn knowledge and ideas into action to solve real-world problems. The ECE sector is very much made up of small business owners. This business side of ECE is important and yet too often overlooked (Stoney & Blank, 2011). ECE offers few professional development opportunities or systems for developing business and entrepreneurial skills and mindsets.

In addition, entrepreneurial leadership is defined not only by traditional notions of risk-taking individuals seeking a profit. Increasingly, people are recognizing that social and educational entrepreneurship is a collaborative, relational, and collective process for improving social aims (Montgomery, Dacin, & Dacin, 2012). In this context, the insights of those closest to the direct work are often essential to innovation. Furthermore, as Couros (2015) asserts, "Innovation is not reserved for the few; it is something we all need to embrace if we are to move forward" (p. 5). It is time to consider embracing the entrepreneurial leadership of early educators as a potentially transformative force for our field.

Design Thinking and Creative Mindsets

The insights from human-centered design offer further guidance about leadership for change and innovation. The design world talks about the mindsets of creative leaders. These are things such as optimism, creative confidence, embracing ambiguity, and empathy (IDEO, 2015). David Kelley is the founder and Tom Kelley is a partner of IDEO, a world-famous global design company. They teach that "creative confidence is about believing in your ability to create change in the world around you" (Kelley & Kelley, 2012). Assuming a beginner's mindset is a core philosophy of design thinking. A beginner's mindset is like a young child's mindset: curious, open to new information and endless possibility, imaginative, and not constrained by what we already know. This mindset is the same one we cherish in young children, but have not paid much attention to when it comes to training and supporting our workforce. Design thinking also shares similarities with relational leadership. It elevates the experiences and expertise of "users"—the people who are the consumers of our services. For example, if we are thinking about how to design and deliver ECE professional development, the "users" are early educators, and their perspectives and needs would drive the design of these services.

It makes sense to cultivate and support these kinds of creative leadership and mindsets in ECE. We can design leadership development programs and systems that strengthen and reward this kind of bold, creative, innovative leadership. Many early educators are drawn to this field because of their love for young children's creative and imaginative minds. If you have ever been to the exhibit hall at one of the big early childhood education professional conferences, you'll remember the make-and-take craft tables. There is often standing room only at these booths, which are crowded with educators making crowns, tiaras, or flags with glitter, glue, and all kinds of collage materials. We are a creative bunch! This is one reason innovation and entrepreneurial leadership is a good fit. In fact, the innovation world is taking some lessons from us about the importance of play. For example, Stanford University's design school created a course on play that teaches students how to use play to promote innovation in the corporate world. When we unleash our creative energies to pursue better solutions, we open the door to new possibilities for ourselves and our field. As an early educator in one of my classes reflected, "As leaders, we need to follow that inner voice and not block it out with doubt, skepticism, and becoming bogged down in what is believed to be possible. I truly believe that we need to be more like NASA engineers and ask *how* we do something, not *is it possible.*"

THE POSSIBILITIES OF EARLY EDUCATOR LEADERSHIP

The traditionally masculine-gendered notions of individualistic, heroic, and entrepreneurial leadership raise many questions about how to move forward. How should we make sense of these varied and gendered ideas? As noted above, some have called for ECE to adopt a form of relational leadership that aligns with the caring, collaborative aspects of our field; others are concerned that this approach reinforces the idea of a distinctly feminine form of leadership. Would that maintain the marginalization of women's work and women's leadership? What is most interesting is that, increasingly, strong and effective leadership is defined across industries by collaborative, inclusive, and relational practices.

These seismic shifts in how good leadership is now defined and practiced align strongly with decades of calls for relational and collaborative leadership in ECE. As we redefine leadership in these more modern, inclusive, and relational ways, we can see the possibilities for the leadership of early educators. This has happened for countless educators and students with whom I've worked. Redefining leadership in relational ways has led them to identify as leaders, often for the first time. An educator, a former student of mine, shared this story about coming to see herself as a leader.

> I learned that I'm good at achieving consensus. I want to take everyone's thoughts and feelings into account before I move forward. I never was comfortable just dictating and making a decision. But in previous experiences I've been criticized for that. I was too feminine almost; I was not strong enough because maybe a man would just decide. In learning about leadership, I realized that my way is actually a really great way to lead. So I didn't ever feel bad about that again. This is my leadership style.

She developed her strengths for leading change to improve ECE. She started this process by redefining what leadership means, and she began to see herself as a leader for the first time. We must create opportunities and possibilities for early educators to see themselves and others as leaders.

Redefining leadership may help early educators see themselves as leaders, but broader public recognition of early educator leadership continues to be wanting. At times, I have encountered skepticism from those within and outside of our field about early educators' capacity to be leaders and change agents. Much of this skepticism is likely driven by the low status afforded the field and the caring nature of the work. Therefore, it is important to target and disrupt these negative stereotypes.

I have been in more than one meeting where people were talking about improving early education by building data systems to track children and see how they develop and learn. In these meetings, I have noticed that whenever people talk about a data system, they talk about "a smart data person" or getting someone "supersmart" to build it. No one ever talks about supersmart early educators. They attach the word *smart* only when they talk about "data people." People apparently believe that understanding numbers and computers involves more intelligence than understanding child development, learning, and relationships. I argue that the situation is just the opposite. I have started to add the word *smart* as often as possible when I talk about educators.

I was struck when I heard an Early Head Start system administrator do just this at a meeting. She beautifully modeled what it looks like to recognize and respect early educators' expertise and leadership. She was meeting with a group of 20 child-care center directors to work on their implementation of an Early Head Start Child-Care partnership whose goal was to improve the quality of infant–toddler child care. She told the directors, "When you're innovating a new model, this is what it looks like: You bring a group of geniuses together, and you figure it out." By "geniuses," she meant all the child-care directors in the room, who were engaging with her in a collaborative process of identifying solutions to overcome the seemingly intractable barriers to quality improvement.

The complexity of early educators' work, and their unique expertise, must be recognized and valued more widely. Lee Shulman, a professor at Stanford University who has been studying teaching for more than 30 years, demonstrates a deep appreciation for educators' highly skilled work. He concludes that teaching

> is perhaps the most complex, most challenging, and most demanding, subtle, nuanced, and frightening activity that our species has ever invented. . . . The only time a physician could possibly encounter a situation of comparable complexity would be in the emergency room of a hospital during or after a natural disaster. (Shulman, Wilson, & Hutchings, 2004, p. 504)

Early educators possess the professional insight, expertise, and passion that we know make a difference. Bringing the possibility of early educator leadership to the forefront is a transformative act in and of itself.

CONCLUSION

Research on relational and entrepreneurial leadership offers important evidence that creative and innovative leadership can result in transformative change, moving beyond the status quo. These forms of leadership can expand the ways the ECE sector imagines the possibilities of leadership and leadership development. In addition, this research shows the importance of leadership development that includes supports for entrepreneurial activity. K–12 education has a robust literature on teacher leadership, and ECE must take a bold step in this direction (Lieberman, Campbell, & Yashkina, 2017). It is time to embark on a new era of leadership development research, practice, and policy in ECE.

CHAPTER 4

Leading Change, Improvement, and Innovation

What if early education were the most respected and revered profession in America? It most definitely warrants this distinction, and it's time to push forward. What other profession yields a $10 or more return for every $1 invested? This is an exciting time of transformation in the field of early care and education. The positive impact of early educators' work with young children and their families increasingly is recognized by policymakers, economists, and the public. Early educators can be the engine for innovation, but they have been overlooked when it comes to leading change. Experienced early educators can feel frustrated and demoralized by the lack of advanced professional development opportunities. Many are weary of yet another mandated change pushed down into ECE programs without sufficient resources. And many have ideas, expertise, and passion, and are hungry for an opportunity to strengthen the profession and make an even bigger difference in the lives of children and families.

Experienced early educators are an untapped lever for improving quality and generating innovations. This chapter synthesizes the key lessons and insights from the previous chapters about new ways to close the persistent gaps in opportunity for young children, nurture leadership from within the field, and cultivate a professional culture of excellence and innovation.

A PARADIGM SHIFT

The previous chapters presented theory and research evidence from across many different sectors. Theories of change are informed by the scientific study of organizational systems and cultures, relational dynamics, and innovation mindsets. We learned that leadership for change, informed by relational, entrepreneurial, and feminist leadership scholarship, looks very different from the traditional notions of leadership. Bringing so many different theories and bodies of research to the table might seem overwhelming. But the most amazing thing about this journey across disciplines is the common thread throughout about what it really takes to make change work. Figure 4.1 pulls out

Figure 4.1. Assumptions and Beliefs About Leadership and Change

Key Dimensions of Leadership & Change	Traditional Approach	Relational & Systems Approach
Source of expertise, ideas, solutions	External experts Narrowly defined	Internal and external experts Broadly defined
Driver of change	Formal leadership, experts, regulatory authorities	Those closest to the work, educators, families
Relationships	Hierarchical	Reciprocal, mutual, respectful, across roles
Focus for change	Individuals	Whole systems
Organizational culture	Compliance	Learning
Role of formal leaders	Managers	Facilitators
Role of educators in change	Adopters Passive	Leaders Co-creators

those common themes. It contrasts the dominant approaches to leadership and change with the relational systems approach described in this book. It helps us to visualize and compare the differing assumptions and beliefs represented in the research and theory about leadership and change.

These differing assumptions underlie the way people design professional development training, programs, and quality improvement interventions and systems. The traditional approach gets in the way of early educator leadership for change. It excludes the possibility that educators possess the expertise and insight necessary to drive change and innovate. In contrast, the relational and systems approach makes that possibility visible and creates opportunities for this leadership to flourish.

FIVE REASONS TO DEVELOP LEADERSHIP FOR CHANGE

Modern definitions of leadership emphasize a collaborative and relational form of leadership that can be exercised by people in any role or level of an organization or a system. Leading does not require a job title. The research on leadership and change highlights new ways of thinking about what is needed in order to nurture a strong, diverse, resilient workforce to lead change, improvement, and innovation. It points to five compelling reasons to expand the way we think about strengthening our field and improving quality. These five reasons reflect the relational systems approach portrayed in Figure 4.1. Leadership development, particularly entrepreneurial leadership development, is truly the next frontier in ECE.

1. Early Educators Can Lead Change. Leadership and innovation are key drivers of success across sectors, and have been shown to dramatically improve children's learning in K–12 education. Leadership focused on change and innovation can reap similarly dramatic benefits in the early care and education sector. Experienced early educators possess unique insights and expertise that position them to lead change and innovation. Furthermore, the ECE sector itself is uniquely conducive to entrepreneurial growth and innovation, as it is largely a small business sector, led primarily by women and minority business owners, who can operate with high levels of autonomy. This creates opportunities to experiment and test new ideas and solutions.

2. The ECE Sector Lacks Leadership Pathways. Elevating educators' leadership is a missing component of most of our current approaches to workforce development and quality improvement. Almost no opportunities or systems currently exist to develop leadership for improvement and innovation in ECE. Unlike in many other professions, experienced early educators lack opportunities to grow throughout their careers and develop the skills and supports they need to lead in their classrooms, organizations, communities, and beyond. We are losing much-needed talent as a result. A field that fails to nurture leadership from within can drive experienced and innovative thinkers away, depriving us of our richest resource: the talent and innovative ideas of experienced educators. The low wages of early educators often force them to leave the field or to seek second jobs, public assistance, or loans to make ends meet.

3. We Can Make Change Better and More Sustainable. Research on change suggests we can do much better when it comes to improving quality in ECE. For example, while most professional development investments focus on training individual teachers or directors, the science of improvement suggests that collaborative and organizational approaches are far more effective. Teachers do not work in isolation, and when it comes to change, systems thinking reminds us that we must approach change in a holistic way to create a context that supports the new practices. Relational organizational theory shows us how organizational performance depends on positive relationships among all those who work together. Strengthening relationships of mutual respect is an essential foundation for effective organizational change.

These insights call for a paradigm shift from individually oriented quality improvement and professional development to collaborative, workplace-embedded, evidence-based approaches to professional learning. To implement changes in practice requires targeting both the content knowledge (for example, literacy) and methods for improvement. Strengthening workplace relationships must be part of that process. The "how" to change is as important as the "what" (content) to change. This requires bringing together professional development and quality improvement services and resources, and fundamentally shifting at least some of the ways the field supports change.

Typically, professional development and quality improvement operate as two different systems, in silos. They rarely work together or in ways that include educators' and administrators' workplace contexts. For example, as Michael Fullan (2008) attests, "We should not have leadership development programs for individuals in the absence of parallel strategies focusing on changing the culture of school systems. It will take the combined efforts of both components. . . . Individual and organizational development must go hand in hand" (para. 12). When it comes to change and improvement, we must address the systems and contextual factors that enable or prevent the transfer of knowledge into practice, so that we can close the gap between what we know and what we do.

4. Relationships and Respect Matter. The other key insight about change is that relationships and respect matter. Caring and respect are at the core of early childhood teaching, but disrespecting educators in the workplace or having them experience a negative workplace culture can interfere with their capacity to do their job well. Relationships of shared power and mutual respect are the foundation for developing leadership within ECE and for driving better solutions for our field.

This will require moving beyond the status quo in quality improvement and professional development in ECE. Many systems we still use today are broken. Very often, efforts to improve quality in ECE come from outsiders who define the problem and identify its solution. We then often require educators to implement that solution with fidelity—which means to implement it exactly the way the manual describes. These approaches often do not meet educators' needs. The assumption that drives this approach is that expertise is held by others, not by educators. This is a narrow definition of expertise that lifts up researchers' and curriculum developers' expertise while devaluing the expertise that educators and parents bring. What is more, accountability is seen as a one-way street. Educators and ECE program administrators must be accountable to regulatory agencies, but what about the accountability of our systems to meet educators' needs?

The paradigm shift flips the definition of expertise, from knowledge held by a few to knowledge broadly held, with many different people and groups bringing unique expertise that is needed in order to inform better solutions to persistent challenges. It turns accountability into a reciprocal relationship, where each party is accountable to the others to achieve the shared goal of access to high-quality ECE for all children and families. Educators' and ECE program administrators' voices and perspectives are elevated and respected. Without this authentic respect for the expertise and insights educators can bring, this approach is not possible and innovation and improvement will be limited.

5. The Impact Will Be Immense. Early educators are the largest and most racially and linguistically diverse teaching workforce in America. Each week, more than 11 million children ages 0–5 are cared for by early educators, often 5 full days a week, year-round. When we build talent from within this powerful and diverse workforce, we tap into the passion, insight, and leadership that can open doors of opportunity for young children across the nation. Recognizing and elevating early educators' expertise and leadership strengthens our field and advances our professionalism. When we build entrepreneurial leadership here, we retain urgently needed talent in the field, and we seed sustainable change and innovation for future generations.

CONCLUSION

The complex and persistent challenges we face call for creative solutions, informed and driven by early educators. As my colleague Jody Hoffer Gittell (2016) writes, "We must move beyond the idea that leaders are born, and ask instead how we can develop people's capacity to lead" (p. 58). We know what it will take to develop, support, and sustain early educators as change agents and advocates for young children, their families, and the profession. Doing this will require a paradigm shift in the way we think about improvement and change in ECE. This chapter identified five compelling reasons to expand the way we think about strengthening our field and improving quality. To build a strong foundation for leadership from within the field, we need to focus on developing and elevating early educator leadership, improving the ways we go about making change, and building leadership pathways in the field.

There is perhaps nothing more frustrating than a call for action with no concrete strategies or processes for that action. The next chapter highlights what this new leadership and change paradigm might look like in practice, with real educators in real-world settings. Educators and other early childhood professionals are already testing new strategies and innovations in practice. Some of the greatest advances have come from shining a light on how people are already doing things differently, learning from that, and achieving better results. I share lessons and findings from several projects and research studies I've conducted over the past decade. These case studies of leadership and change in ECE illustrate new and promising approaches to nurturing the leadership ECE needs today and for the future. Each of these approaches shares these common characteristics: mutual respect, valuing early educators' expertise, and embedding educator leadership into professional development and quality improvement programming and systems.

Part II

LEADERSHIP PATHWAYS

CHAPTER 5

The Possibilities of Early Educator Leadership

We are at a point in our profession where we need to expand and deepen our thinking about leadership and get concrete about how to transform leadership development accordingly. Early educators' leadership is an issue that has long been debated and discussed. As described earlier, many have called for more leadership development for decades, but the response has been limited. In addition, there has been a lively discussion about barriers to leadership, in particular the potential conflict between the dominant notions of leadership and the kind of leadership that fits the ECE context.

This chapter delves into stories and experiences of early educators as they developed their own leadership identities. It offers concrete strategies for developing one's identity as a leader. It describes a new leadership development program for experienced early educators launched in 2012 at UMass Boston, seeded by a Race to the Top Early Learning Challenge grant provided by the state of Massachusetts. Sharing early educators' leadership stories contributes to a new and powerful narrative about leadership in our field. Also in this chapter, I offer ideas about what each of you can do individually or collectively to make the leadership of early educators stronger and more visible.

BELIEVING

A first step in this process is our believing that we can make something happen, that we can lead change. Early educators' leadership continues to be largely invisible both to the public and within our field. Professional development books, resources, and systems often neglect completely or give little attention to leadership. Professional development systems place a great deal of emphasis on entry-level or minimum credentials for the field without giving comparable attention to how to support experienced members. This is shortsighted. I participated in several recent state and national ECE workforce policy dialogues that contained no mention of leadership until I raised the issue. For example, I met with a diverse group of individuals from across several different sectors who were committed to ECE workforce development and compensation reforms. They asked me to review the draft of their statement about how to transform the workforce. That statement made no mention of leadership. The group members seemed stunned when they realized that they had completely neglected leadership. In fact, many of them were leaders in their own organizations, yet had not seen leadership as relevant or applicable to ECE. The fact that almost every other sector has a leadership development infrastructure of some sort speaks volumes.

It appears that many people may not be able to imagine what early educator leadership looks like. Even within ECE circles, research has indicated that educators themselves do not often consider leadership a defining aspect of their professional identity. This invisibility is linked to many societal and economic factors, such as the low status society affords to this field and gender stereotypes about leadership.

Due to these factors, elevating the visibility of early educator leadership can be a revolutionary act in and of itself. We need to show the world that early educator leadership is possible and that early educators possess unique knowledge and professional insights that are essential for understanding how to change and improve ECE. The change we need must be driven from within our field, informed by this expertise. When change actually results in lasting improvements, it is never something that happens to us: It is always something we make happen. Making this leadership visible can change perceptions—our own and others'—about the possibilities of early educator leadership.

DEVELOPING AS LEADERS

I begin this chapter with a personal story. When I was about 8 years old, I had a minor accident on my roller skates and hurt my knee. When I got home, I told my mother how I had fallen on the bumpy, uneven brick sidewalk in front of a neighbor's house. My mom could have warned me not to skate there again, and she could have comforted me (and she probably did), but that is not what I remember so vividly. In fact, I remember this incident only because of what happened next: My mom suggested that I contact the mayor to report the unsafe condition of the sidewalk and to ask that the city fix it.

With that suggestion, and my 8-year-old outrage about the condition of that sidewalk, I wrote a letter to the mayor. My mom must have been cheering quietly when I received a call from the mayor herself, thanking me for the letter and reporting the good news that the city would be out to fix the sidewalk soon. I share this story for a few reasons. This one incident is something I have remembered my whole life—as a moment in time when I saw the possibilities of taking action to make change, of my power to effect change. I am sure I tried to change many things in my early years, but I remember this time, when my experience enabled me to have an impact on a problem. This success bolstered my confidence that I could make a difference to solve a problem. My mom pointed me toward the possibility that I could make this change happen. Now you know I have an activist for a mother!

So how does this story apply to early educators' leadership development? The story speaks to identity. Our identity is our sense of ourselves, and it is a powerful influence on how we think and act. If we want to support leadership development, we cannot just teach about leadership theory, skills, and competencies. We also must look inward, and help others look inward, to reflect on the unique qualities, experiences, and passions we bring to our work, and to question the barriers or stereotypes that may hold us back individually and collectively. One thing that holds many back from taking action is self-doubt, a doubt in our power to change something. This story illustrates that a first step in leading change is to believe that we can make something happen. We have to be able to see a pathway for ourselves as change agents. Often, that pathway or entry point comes from an everyday experience in which we succeeded in making a difference. What if each of us could find one time when we succeeded in making a change, and then we used that to empower us to change the things we care most about?

LESSONS FROM LEADERSHIP DEVELOPMENT

Why does it matter if early educators identify as leaders? This question is one I continually reflect on as a professor of leadership and policy. While research on ECE leadership is still limited, several recent studies reveal important ways in which leadership identity matters for early educators (Armstrong, Kinney, & Clayton, 2009; Dana & Yendol-Hoppey, 2005; Mevorach & Miron, 2011). When we launched a new leadership development program at UMass Boston in 2012, we partnered with our state to design it as a professional pathway for experienced early educators. The purpose of the new program was to create a leadership pathway for early educators, serve as a pipeline to doctoral programs in early education to stem the shortage of skilled birth-to-5 early education faculty, and expand opportunities to advance leadership for improvement and innovation from within the field.

The UMass Boston leadership program trains educators to use the combined power of research evidence and their professional expertise to drive improvements and innovation in practice and policy. The program was designed to enhance educators' capacity to be change agents—to be the voice in the field advancing change in ways that ensure that all young children and their families thrive. To be eligible for the program, applicants had to be working in the ECE sector. We selected applicants to ensure diverse representation from the ECE sector, including family child-care providers, Head Start teachers, center-based ECE educators, and early educators working in public school settings and early intervention programs. We conducted a study of the program and its first three cohorts (Douglass, 2016a, 2016c). In this chapter, I share key lessons learned from this study. One overarching question investigated in the study was how educators developed their identity as leaders. The findings revealed a pattern in the process of coming to see oneself as a leader in which educators redefined leadership, identified their passion and purpose as leaders, and took action—sometimes one small step to start.

Redefining Leadership

Traditional notions of leadership have been associated with stereotypically male traits and behaviors. Research shows that women face many barriers when it comes to developing as leaders and obtaining positions of leadership. Educators in the UMass Boston leadership program almost always started their leadership journey by redefining leadership. Many, strongly identifying with contemporary notions of leadership as highly relational and collaborative, focused on influencing positive change for the field. One educator and owner of a child-care center shared this about her leadership journey:

> My previous career was in the technology repair industry. I felt the full lash of institutionalized sexism and racism. After 7 years, I left the industry because who I am as a person was not a match for expectations due to my proclivity to favor relational leadership. Kindness can be confused with weakness in predominantly masculine groups. Now I work with 16 females and one male teacher. The dynamics are very different. Leadership that empowers is essential. Being self-employed allows me the autonomy to create the environment I want to work in. I no longer have to worry if my kindness will be mistaken for weakness. I cannot be in every classroom to monitor teachers and their interactions, nor do I want to be. I have a highly empowered group of professionals that really don't need me to be there in order to function.

This educator identified as a relational leader, but found that not everyone welcomed or respected that kind of leadership when she worked in the technology sector. She made a career change years ago into ECE and has found success leading a high-quality child-care program by empowering and respecting teachers' expertise. She identifies as an educator and entrepreneurial business owner who is drawn to the autonomy in ECE that enables her to be creative in designing and managing her program. For her, the concept of entrepreneurial leadership resonated and helped her to define herself as a leader.

Another key theme that emerged in this study of educator leadership development was that educator expertise is essential to effective leadership for change, as reflected by one educator: "A lot of people who are making the decisions for the field are not experienced in the field. I think that we need to get leadership from those of us who have had the experience, have been in the classroom . . . so, a more bottom-up approach to leadership." Educators' expertise was an asset for their leadership. It filled a gap left by a tendency for those unfamiliar with the work to be in positions of authority in ECE systems. The family child-care providers in the leadership program gave similar feedback about their experience. Diane, a family child-care provider and business owner for more than 20 years, said that her experience in the program "inspired me to be a leader for change in my profession." She described how impactful it was that I, as her professor, worked as a family child-care provider myself in the past and talked in class about my experiences as a provider. Diane shared, "When she [my professor] disclosed that she had worked in family child care, it inspired me to expand my own career path. As a student in her class, it made me relax and feel the powerful effect of sharing experiences with her" (Douglass, Benson, et al., 2015, p. 15).

Once educators redefined leadership in collaborative, relational, and purpose-driven ways, they could connect these new theories of leadership to their own past, present, and future actions and capabilities. This enabled them to identify as leaders, often for the first time, as summed up by one educator: "Through my journey in the program, I learned not only what it means to be a great leader in the field of early education, but that I am capable of being that great leader." They gained confidence about their leadership, as this ECE director's experience reflects: "Who knows, maybe our directors' group can contribute to a movement that helps to lead change rather than one that helps others to tolerate it." Her identity as a leader expanded. She came to see herself and her colleagues as people who could take charge and lead change, rather than be the object of change. She came to think of change itself in a new way, too—not as something to tolerate, but as a powerful tool for strengthening our field and ECE quality.

The importance of developing a leadership identity is supported in other research, including research on women's leadership. Ely, Ibarra, and Kolb (2011) describe how gender shapes women's pathways into leadership, arguing that a leadership identity is the foundation for leadership development. Given that dominant notions of leadership often conform to societal stereotypes about men, they argue that leadership identity must be the foundation of women's leadership development. They highlight how this identity then strengthens women's confidence as leaders: "An elevated sense of purpose challenges leaders to move outside of their comfort zones, shifts their attention from what is to what is possible, and gives them a compelling reason to face down their fears and insecurities and take action despite them" (p. 476). The famous social psychologist Albert Bandura (1977) coined the term *self-efficacy*, which refers to this belief in oneself and one's capacity to exercise influence and succeed in one's efforts.

The story of Becky, an early educator and former student of mine, illustrates the process of coming to see oneself as a leader. Becky's leadership journey ultimately resulted in her changing something she had wanted to change for a long time but had never had the courage or the confidence to try. She had been an early educator for 19 years and had always been passionate about working with young children. When she entered the leadership program, she was a teacher in the 3-year-old class at a laboratory preschool, and then she was promoted to an interim director position while her program hired a permanent director.

One of the most powerful experiences for Becky in coming to see herself as a leader was something called the Reflected Best Self Exercise (RBSE), a leadership development assignment I use in my leadership course. Developed by professors at the University of Michigan business school (Quinn, Dutton, Spreitzer, & Roberts, 2011), its purpose is to discover the unique and distinctive strengths, qualities, and capabilities that enable us to be at our best. It helps us build on these strengths and learn how to surround ourselves with the things that bring out those greatest strengths.

The RBSE is based on the belief, supported by scientific evidence, that each person's greatest room for growth is in the areas of their unique strengths or special talents. Research has shown that when we develop a sense of our best possible self, we can better make and lead positive change. The way this exercise works is that you ask 10 to 20 people to write about three occasions when people saw you at your best. Additionally, you write your own reflections on three occasions when you were at your best. Then you collect all these stories and search for common themes among them, looking for recurring behaviors and patterns. When I use this exercise in my course, I next ask my students, all early educators, to create a portrait of their "best self," using any form or format they choose. They do all kinds of portraits: video, painting, poem, sculpture, narrative, dance, or other form of representation.

Becky made a nest for her portrait (see Figure 5.1). She created it by cutting into strips the best self stories she'd collected. Each strip contained words and reflections on her strengths and unique contributions. She used papier-mâché to combine, overlap, and weave the stories together into this nest. She presented her portrait to the class, explaining, "I wanted to create a piece that shows the interconnectedness of the stories; thus I used 33 individual strands of fishing line to represent the number of stories I received, and 11 brightly colored beads, one for each of the respondents. I hoped to create something that was three-dimensional and represented a vessel

Figure 5.1. Becky's Nest

for my own growth as a leader. I chose an open vessel to communicate my openness to new stories, experiences, and relationships."

Becky's nest symbolizes her unique qualities and her emerging leadership. A nest is a home, a safe place to grow and develop as a leader, and a launching pad for taking a risk—and learning to fly. Becky said that this exercise changed the way she viewed herself as a leader in ways that empowered her. She hung the nest on her wall so she can be reminded of this every day.

So many of the educators in my classes have found this to be a transformative exercise. One worked as an early educator coach, and she reflected on her leadership development in this way:

> My strength is in inspiring and motivating others to follow their own dreams. As I connect with people, I foster their own discovery of the resources and answers hidden within them. I'm a coach and guide. It [the RBSE] connected me with the core of who I am, and I feel like I can take on the world.

Imagine you asked 10 people who know you well (your boss, coworkers, parents, friends, family) to write about three times when they saw you at your best. Imagine writing your own best self stories. What are your greatest strengths and qualities that you might discover in those stories? How could you use that knowledge and insight about your unique contributions and special talents to change you and strengthen you as a leader?

In Becky's words, this is what she learned:

> I am worthy. I have a place. I may not be an imposter after all. The Reflected Best Self Exercise taught me about my place in the world,

> and in the field of early childhood education. The stories that were written for me showed me that I truly belong here. I make a difference.

Respect for early educators' contributions and expertise is powerful. We need much more of it. We need to spread and cultivate this respect. One family child-care provider in our leadership program shared this reflection: "Being part of this leadership program is the first time in my career that I, as a family child-care provider, have felt my work and my contribution have been recognized and valued by others." It is time to elevate and respect the expertise of early educators and value their contributions to our children and our economy.

Identifying Passion and Purpose

Another common theme that emerged from the study of this program was passion and purpose. Educators talked about the importance of identifying what they were most passionate about, where their greatest and most unique strengths lay, and focusing their leadership on that one area. This was particularly important for educators who did not have formal leadership roles. It helped them define what leadership meant for them as a teacher or family child-care provider. As they identified the change and improvement they wanted to see in the field, their leadership took on a purpose that gave many the courage to take action and risks they previously would not have considered.

Becky's new confidence about her leadership enabled her to take action on an idea she had had for a while. She told me that one of the most important lessons she learned was this: "I shouldn't let my ideas just be inklings, but I should really let them blossom." So she let one of her ideas blossom: She launched a program she called "Real Art for Real Children." She had always wanted to do this as a teacher, to bring in a real artist once a month for children. She was passionate about art. She wanted children to see that even when you're a grown-up, you can still be an artist. Art is not just child's play. She told me, "So now every month we have a grown-up come in—an artist—and do their grown-up art so it's not a preschool lesson. It's grown-ups actually doing it with all their sharp tools and hot objects."

Becky took on a new leadership role outside her preschool. She became a member of a statewide early childhood advisory committee—a leadership opportunity she described as something she really had never seen herself doing because, as she said, "I didn't know that I had anything to offer." Now she knows otherwise! She has so much to offer, and her strengths and wisdom as a leader have been unleashed.

Becky was continuing as the interim center director for the rest of the year, but she wanted to return to the classroom as soon as possible. "When I'm too old to get up off the floor, then maybe being the director would be cool. But for now, I still want to be teaching children. I still feel like I have so much more to learn. And so many more ideas to try. It's a special thing to feel really called to your work."

Becky's story offers key insights about leadership development. Through the leadership program and the Reflected Best Self Exercise, Becky came to believe enough in herself, and in her idea, to take action and do something. This was an idea she had had for a while, one that was sitting there inside her, but she hadn't nurtured it, shared it, or put it into action until she came to see herself as a leader, until she discovered her best self. It is a powerful act to unleash this leadership and make it visible. We can't nurture and grow what we can't see. We can't expect others to commit to and invest in what they can't see. We simply must make early educator leadership more visible.

We can see from Becky's story how powerful it is when individuals come to see the possibilities of their own leadership. The RBSE is one way educators connect with their strengths and unique talents to uncover new possibilities for their leadership. Often, they are profoundly moved by the way people write about them in the best self stories they solicited from colleagues, friends, parents, and other family members. Educators often reflect on our tendency to undervalue our leadership qualities or to see them as deficits. They often come to see that their intensity is passion, their stubbornness is persistence, and their far-fetched ideas are courageous and bold.

Taking Action

Developing one's identity and passions as a leader with a purpose is transformative and life-changing. But it goes beyond individual transformation and empowerment. Becky's story reveals another important insight: that identifying yourself as a purposeful leader can act as a catalyst to action. What's more, believing in your idea, and having others begin to believe in it, can be transformative.

Amanda entered the graduate certificate program at UMass Boston with 20 years' experience and a diverse professional background. Her experiences

Leadership Reflection Questions

- What if we believed we were as strong as others see us? What would we do differently?
- Do you have an idea you have been thinking about for a while?
- What is something you are passionate about changing?
- What happens when we step outside of our comfort zone?
- What are the possibilities for your leadership?

as an actor, artist, preschool educator, and early childhood administrator shaped her unique perspective and research interests. She was particularly interested in children's imaginative play.

As Amanda began her research about creativity and imaginative play, she realized that not a lot of research dealt specifically with her interests. She designed a research project that would support teachers' understanding of young children's imaginations and dramatic play. While designing her study, she began to think about teachers' own imaginations and the contexts in which teachers work. How would they be able to support children's imaginative play and creative thinking if they did not have opportunities to engage their own creative thinking skills? She searched the ECE literature, but couldn't find a common definition of what imagination was or concrete strategies for educators to use in cultivating imagination and creativity with children.

So Amanda developed a plan to design an assessment of imaginary play in early childhood classrooms. It would not only define imaginative play, but also provide a resource for teachers so that they could evaluate their classrooms' capacity to support creative and imaginative thinking. She became so immersed in this work that she applied to and entered an early childhood education PhD program and is investing in her research on this topic full-time. She is well on her way as a trailblazer in supporting the ways that teachers nurture children's creative thinking and imaginative play, especially by nurturing it within themselves.

When we allow students of any age to engage in inquiry and follow their own path to learning, the result can be amazing. Passion and purpose are unleashed, fueling action to lead change and build the confidence to create and innovate. It is a powerful act when we encourage educators to ask, "What if . . . ?" and doggedly pursue the answer.

Becky and Amanda are inspiring educators and leaders. But make no mistake: They did not always identify as leaders. They came to see themselves as leaders through leadership training, mutual support, and networking. Leadership did not come easily or even naturally to them. They began to build a leadership network while in the program, and upon graduation they reached out to expand their networks to help them pursue changes to strengthen ECE. As one educator explained, it takes self-confidence to put oneself out there and be proactive in utilizing networks to drive change. This educator noted that the program "emphasized the thought that 'you are a leader, so just go for it!' and that is what gave me the confidence to contact [a statewide nonprofit entity] and say, 'I'm the expert in this.'" This educator has now launched an innovative pilot ECE program made possible through partnership with that entity. Through these networks, early educators have been able to access resources, information, and sometimes funding to help achieve their goals.

These early educators sometimes doubted themselves and their ideas, and they were not always sure what the next step was. Amanda, for example, had such a big idea it was at times overwhelming. It is not always easy to take that first step to act. In fact, planning a major step can be daunting, even paralyzing, and can become a barrier to action. I address this directly in the leadership courses I teach. Many educators in the leadership program have found it helpful to think about small steps, as well as big steps. Your first step does not have to be a big one. To illustrate, I share the following exercise that I use with groups of early educators.

Imagine, for example, that you want to improve family-engagement practices where you work, and that I have asked you to identify all the things that need to happen to achieve your goal. You might include in your list some big things: You might need money, you might want to change a government policy, or you might want everyone involved to be on board and working together to make the change. Those are important, long-term things that might take a while. There are also many other steps that require far less time, such as convening a parent meeting or conducting a parent survey. We sometimes forget about the smaller changes, leaving us immobilized.

In my leadership course, I do an exercise where teachers brainstorm all the things that would need to happen in order to improve something. They write down their ideas on little sticky notes. Then I ask them to organize the sticky notes into three piles: things that will take a long time (over a year), things that can be done in a few months, and things that can be done by next Friday.

This exercise helps us overcome one of the biggest barriers to leading change: that it's overwhelming, and we don't have control over what needs to change. It turns out that there are always ideas in that pile of things that can be done by next Friday. That means we can do something. Scientific evidence confirms that small changes can make a big difference. If you do something small, something within your immediate reach, and it works, you have just had a success. Success is energizing. It can start what's called the snowball effect, where small changes start to create a momentum that fuels bigger changes.

I have found that educators very often have ideas, big and small, and that many benefit from scaffolded supports to nurture these ideas and take action. In my leadership course, I assign the children's book *What Do You Do with an Idea?* by Kobi Yamada (2013). The book tells the story of a child who has an idea that some might consider crazy, wild, or scary. At first, the child tries to ignore the idea. But over time, the child learns to value and embrace the idea, develop and grow it. The child explains, "I liked being with my idea. It made me feel more alive, like I could do anything. It encouraged me to think big . . . and then, to think bigger." This powerful story has resonated with the educators I teach and inspired them to embrace and explore their own ideas that very often have the potential to transform. This kind of entrepreneurial leadership training cultivates mindsets, strategies, and methods for managing, growing, and unleashing big ideas in concrete ways.

CONCLUSION

Some experienced educators who were on the brink of leaving the field have stayed, and they now possess a renewed commitment and a pathway forward for their leadership. Leadership development programs can unleash this passion and talent and can establish leadership networks to spark and sustain change. The early educators who graduated from this leadership program are leading change at every level. More than half of recent graduates have taken on new jobs or serve on statewide advisory boards. Several have already launched innovative early childhood model programs or entered doctoral programs to become leading researchers, policy advocates, and teacher educators. Leadership development is a key strategy for retaining diverse, experienced, and talented educators in the field, and for building critical capacity for advancing quality early learning experiences for young children.

Leadership for change is action-oriented. In taking action, we strengthen our own confidence in, and knowledge of, the many ways we can drive change to improve opportunities for young children and their families.

In promoting the leadership of others, or as leaders ourselves, we can all take three important steps:

1. We must work harder to ensure that early educators' leadership is visible, accessible to all, and supported.
2. We must cultivate respect for this leadership and for early educators' knowledge and expertise.
3. We must take action and do something to make positive change happen.

CHAPTER 6

Building Leadership Pathways

We have seen how early educators can develop their identity as leaders by redefining leadership in more relational and collaborative ways. Once educators see their own potential to lead, they often identify a passion and purpose that will fuel their leadership for change. The educators in the UMass Boston leadership certificate program came to see themselves as leaders who wanted to make their visions and plans for change a reality after graduation. Many searched for ongoing leadership pathways that might offer a set of next steps and supportive resources to enable them to continue to work toward their goal. A few readily found such pathways, others built them, and some struggled to find the right path that aligned with their needs and interests.

This chapter examines leadership pathways, drawing from the research literature and the results from the study of the UMass Boston program. Leadership and professional pathways serve several purposes. They offer a set of steps one can take to reach a professional milestone or goal, and they support educators' movement into leadership positions, much like a pipeline that provides visibility into how one advances in the field. This chapter explores how educators took action as change agents and how they defined and co-created professional and leadership pathways to pursue their purpose. Their insights and experiences point to a set of concrete supports that need to be put into place more systemically. Leadership pathways must be visible, so that early educators can see the opportunities and access them. In addition, we need to expand the way we think about and strengthen leadership pathways in our field.

TAKING ACTION TO LEAD CHANGE

I followed the experiences of the educators in the UMass Boston leadership certificate program after they graduated. These educators were emerging teacher-leaders who brought a deep understanding of practice to their leadership for change. This program was designed to help build pathways for early educators to lead, from their classrooms to ECE programs, their communities, and beyond. Through our study, the program team wanted to learn how early educators took action to drive changes and what facilitated or hindered their efforts. We wanted to understand ways we might strengthen or expand or shift our work in order to create a greater support system for their leadership once they graduated. My research team and I examined the written assignments and change plans submitted by each educator, conducted a survey of graduates, and held in-depth interviews with individual educators about a year after they graduated. In these interviews, educators talked about their experiences in the program, their professional and leadership goals, the impact of the program on their professional practice and activities, and their leadership pathway. We learned what they wanted to change, how they were trying to make that change happen, and some early signs of impact from their leadership.

These educators reported a wide range of leadership activities, which included professional advancement, such as searching for new jobs and applying to doctoral programs, and making changes to improve practice and/or policy. These educators sought to deepen their impact by leading specific improvements within their workplace or through procuring new professional positions. The study found that as a result of their leadership development and access to supportive networks, educators took actions to position themselves to have a deeper or broader impact on ECE in five different ways (Douglass, 2016a, 2016c).

Leading Change at Work

While some educators pursued new jobs or doctoral programs, others focused on implementing change where they currently worked. For example, one educator, whose focal area was family engagement, created a welcoming family space at her program and changed the morning drop-off protocols to allow parents to come into the building and have an opportunity to speak with teachers. She explained:

> The room next door is our family room. We didn't have a family room [before]. And that's huge. And absolutely that came from my experience in the program. We also changed our drop-off. Our parents used to drop off outside, and their children would walk in alone. It never felt warm; it never felt welcoming. I can remember seeing parents stopping at that second door and peeking around. And I thought, "Absolutely not." So again, and it was met with much resistance, but in the [leadership program] we talked about forging [ahead] and doing what we know is right, and then I think about those books we read [about] leading change. Sometimes you have to just keep moving forward. You can't get stuck on "Does everybody agree? Are we going to do it? Aren't we?" You just have to kinda bulldoze your way through sometimes.

These remarks highlight how one educator accomplished a change that previously had been unachievable. Through her increased confidence, knowledge, and a leadership mindset, she engaged with others in her center and facilitated this change to improve the quality of family engagement in her program.

Another set of changes involved educators' realization that they were being perceived by families differently from how they previously had been perceived. They described feeling more respected by families and being seen as professionals who possessed expertise and knowledge. Some found that parents engaged in more conversation with them about the children, and others found that parents demonstrated a new respect for the "seriousness" with which the educators engaged in the profession. Two students offered similar descriptions of the overall change, noting that having participated in the program created "a different level of expertise" to bring to the families.

Some students emphasized the value of being exposed to research and learning how to benefit from it. They expressed increased confidence in their teaching practices and cited initial associations between their improved practice and children's growth. One student commented:

> So I think what was really influential for me was reading research. Knowing where to find it, knowing how to read it, understand it, knowing if it was valuable. Could I take this and apply it? I think that probably influenced me the most, and still is [influencing me] today. So if I am going to work with a student who is on the spectrum, and I'm wondering, *Okay, how am I going to teach phonological awareness?* I'm researching it now. I'm not just going on Pinterest to find the cutest activity. I'm saying, "Okay, what works? What do we already know works for these children?" So I think that was a huge shift for me, and for a lot of teachers I think. I don't think that's something in the field of early childhood we take advantage of.

These results highlight how educators were equipped with a new sense of confidence in their expertise and leadership, which they gained from the interplay of their experience, passion, and new knowledge, and the supportive relationships and networks formed during the leadership certificate program. They advanced their professionalism in their own eyes and in the eyes of the families they served.

Advancing into New Jobs

Some educators took new jobs to position themselves to make change with a greater impact or scale than would have been possible in their prior jobs. This led to increases in their salaries. For example, two educators moved from working with one class or group of children to leading early childhood services in an entire city or region, multiplying their reach to 20 times more children and families.

One educator, Marla, worked as an early childhood special education coordinator in an elementary school while completing the UMass Boston leadership program. After graduating, she applied for and was hired in a new position as the early childhood special education coordinator for her entire school district. She expanded her reach from 40 children per year to more than 400. She credits her new job to the leadership development program for instilling in her the belief in her own power to make change, implement improvement, and shift the district's culture, which had been devaluing early childhood teachers and family engagement. She had had the personal experience of being dismissed as an early educator. "As a preschool teacher, I have felt disrespected so many times." When she moved to her new job, the early childhood teachers in the district told her they were so hopeful now because "no one listened to us before." One principal told Marla not to worry about what was going on in the pre-K classrooms because "it's just day care." It was obvious to Marla that early childhood education had been marginalized in this district, and administrators and teachers and community-based ECE providers all knew that.

Marla set out to change the culture in the district. She brought together the ECE community with the public schools for joint professional development. She created forums for collaborative professional learning and dialogue, explaining that "really good things happen when you let people's voices be heard." A local ECE director confirmed the transformative effects of Marla's leadership. Marla continues to lead changes. She articulated the urgent need and her commitment to better serve young children with special needs: "We take our most fragile children and we don't serve them well. We could fix this in ways that don't even cost money. The solutions are just as much about will, and the belief that ECE matters—that families must be engaged and respected, and that children with special needs can learn."

Pursuing an Entrepreneurial Venture

Many early educators have pursued entrepreneurial ventures, to imagine something new or different. These educators typically reported that the program supported the development of their ideas and gave them the courage to announce their ideas and seek support for them. Examples of entrepreneurial activities initiated by the educators include contacting foundations and state and nonprofit organizations to present their ideas for new ventures and to seek support for them—for example, establishing a mission-specific school and a STEM preschool, founding an organization to encourage diverse teachers to enter the profession, and developing an app to increase family engagement in toddlers' language development. These educators garnered important support from their cohort and the leadership networks they built while in the program. It took courage for each of them to pursue what was often a big and bold idea.

Taking on a Leadership Role in the Profession

Many educators reported joining new professional associations or advisory boards, and often playing leadership roles. As one said, "I have taken on a lot of roles. [I'm] not just going to work and doing my daily job. I partnered with [the state] and I sit on a committee and we work on changes and revisions for the field." Similarly, another said, "I'm on [state] committees—which is amazing to be able to experience that and see the [state's early education] department and how it works and be part of that work. I'd say that's probably the biggest influence in building my networks. I've had people reach out to *me* from other organizations."

Pursuing Doctoral Study

Several educators reported that they planned to further their academic training by pursuing a PhD. Four have been admitted to and started doctoral programs. "This [leadership] program has helped me open my eyes to how much I want to pursue a PhD—something I'd considered before but did not really think was a reality."

SEEKING AND CO-CREATING LEADERSHIP PATHWAYS

The early educators in this program all sought to follow or create a pathway in the field to advance and to lead, in the diverse array of ways described in this chapter. Those who wanted to pursue a PhD encountered a fairly clear pathway by identifying appropriate program options, applying, and in some cases entering a doctoral program. In fact, this leadership development program was designed to create that pathway from the field into doctoral programs, to grow a new generation of scholar-practitioners with birth-to-5 expertise in early childhood teacher education programs. Others, who sought to drive change within their workplace or to pursue changes beyond that, often confronted challenges in finding a supportive pathway.

Barriers

One of these barriers was the absence of clearly defined leadership development systems and pathways. As one educator explained, "I knew where I wanted to go; I didn't know how to get there. I'm feeling my path, but I'm feeling like I'm blindly feeling it. I'm grabbing at certain things, trying to figure out which path to take. You're hoping that somebody has already taken my path, and you know that's not true." In response to such challenges, many educators spoke about the need to build bridges, individually and collectively, to develop better defined leadership pathways for those in the field. A related barrier was the lack of ongoing professional development offerings for experienced educators. One educator observed, "There are inservice trainings and other forms of professional development, but they are often geared to those who are new to the field. Thus, more experienced teachers often do not have opportunities to grow and develop."

Overall, their comments expressed a sense of frustration that the field offers too few opportunities for upward mobility and advanced professional learning. Educators also spoke about the lack of access to financial resources and professional networks needed to implement and test an innovation or a change. Several educators pursuing innovative and entrepreneurial ventures to achieve change noted the lack of an innovation infrastructure in the field.

Rethinking Leadership Pathways

The lack of a field-wide leadership development system and supports for educator innovation has led many professionals in the field to locate their leadership routes through multiple, often nontraditional, pathways. The traditional understanding of leadership pathways is a sequence of linear steps to formal leadership positions in organizations or systems. While this is an important next step in professional development for the field, it will not solve an important aspect of the problem.

A key theme in this book is that leadership is more than a formal job title: It is a highly relational process of influencing change to achieve a shared goal. When leadership is defined in this way, rather than as a job title, the concept of a leadership pathway necessarily shifts. Rather than a pipeline for advancing into a formal leadership position, it becomes a supportive and ongoing environment, enabling change agents to gain competencies and be effective and successful. A leadership pathway for this kind of leader may look more like a supported and ongoing developmental process.

This reminds me of author Dave Evans, a management consultant and adjunct faculty member at Stanford University, who talks about the concept of "wayfinding" as a strategy for those who feel stuck and unable to see a way forward. In a recent interview on National Public Radio's *Morning Edition,* he explained, "When you can't know what you're doing, you can't navigate like a GPS because you don't have a map, and you don't have all the information: you have to wayfind. And wayfinding means taking one step at a time, knowing something about the direction you're going, trying a few things, tuning it up, and then doing it again and doing it again." Some of the educators I spoke with described exactly this process, and most found it isolating. How can we build a supportive ecosystem for wayfinding, as early educators develop and take action to drive change? We do not need to have or to expect beautifully paved pathways for every kind of leader. Gloria Anzaldúa captures this sense with her words, *Caminante, no hay puentes, se hace puentes al andar* ("Voyager, there are no bridges; one builds them as one walks") (Anzaldúa, Keating, Mignolo, Silverblatt, & Saldívar-Hull, 2009, p. 73).

These conclusions demand a new way of thinking about supporting leadership, one that combines greater access to high-quality leadership development programs, formal leadership pathways and pipelines, and a field-wide leadership development ecosystem that cultivates leadership for change and innovation from within the field. Taking a path that has not been taken before, or trying a new idea, or thinking about problems in new and radical ways, requires creativity and courage. As Tom Kelley and David Kelley write in *Harvard Business Review*, "Creativity is something you practice, not just a talent you're born with" (2012). It is time to cultivate the creativity within our field.

CONCLUSION

This chapter highlights diverse early educators' leadership and points to the kinds of outcomes that are possible. Educators took on leadership to improve early learning opportunities for children and families, and this leadership took many forms.

Forms of Leadership

Leading Change at Work

- Achieving measurable improvement in family-engagement practices
- Designing an app to promote parent-teacher partnerships focused on toddlers' language development

Advancing Professionally

- Moving into a director position
- Assuming leadership of a school district's early childhood special education services

Launching an Entrepreneurial Venture

- Starting up a new model STEM-focused preschool
- Launching a new urban Montessori ECE program

Becoming a Leader in the Profession

- Serving on a statewide early childhood advisory board
- Becoming a mentor to other family child-care providers

Pursuing a PhD

- Applying and entering a doctoral program in ECE or educational leadership

Early educators' leadership holds immense potential to have an impact and transform quality. Many of the educators I have described were inspired and energized as change agents. They stayed in the field as a result, when before they had been discouraged and disheartened about the lack of respect for the profession and the absence of professional supports for experienced educators. Building and co-creating a leadership pathway is exciting, creative, and deeply challenging work. Early educators need access to ongoing supports for their leadership. Other fields have developed an ecosystem that contains supports and resources at multiple levels: program/school, higher education, community, professional association, policy, state, national. These ecosystems have been proven to support professionals to emerge, grow, and thrive as leaders. An example of such an ecosystem can be found in the technology sector. Because leadership for change is inherently relational, we need to develop an ecosystem that supports it, not just an isolated program or individual training program. How to build this ecosystem is the focus of the final Part of this book.

CHAPTER 7

Redesigning Quality Improvement and Professional Development

One way to cultivate diverse leadership within the field is to ensure that early educators have access to leadership development programs and support systems, but that is not the only way to cultivate leadership. Every system or policy that serves our field can be designed in ways that cultivate educator leadership or not. Right now, most of what is offered as quality improvement and professional development shuts out the possibility that early educators can be leaders and agents of change. Educators often are treated as passive adopters of change, rather than as the architects and co-creators of it. Other parts of the economy, such as the health and innovation sectors, have developed methods and strategies for quality improvement and innovation that elevate the expertise and voice of staff as well as that of patients or customers (Berwick, 1994; Gittell, 2016; Langley et al., 2009; Suchman et al., 2014).

As introduced earlier, research shows why it is so important to engage the leadership of those who work most closely with children and families (Gittell, 2016; Suchman et al., 2014). Improvement science is a discipline that studies methods for effectively making improvement and achieving high performance in organizations and systems (Institute for Healthcare Improvement, 2003). The relational organizational research introduced earlier in this book highlights the importance of relationships and shared leadership when it comes to organizational change, yet very little of what is now known about organizational change and transformation has been applied in ECE (Douglass, 2014; Douglass & Gittell, 2012; Eaton, 2000; Gittell, 2016; Glisson & Hemmelgarn, 1998; Golden-Biddle & Mao, 2012). It is time to change that. This chapter describes how these organizational and systems approaches are starting to be applied and how they can make a difference in ECE.

RETHINKING LEADERSHIP IN QUALITY IMPROVEMENT AND PROFESSIONAL DEVELOPMENT

Organizations that respect the expertise of their front-line staff can achieve better outcomes when it comes to quality improvement than those who do not. These organizations and systems retain staff, foster a culture of respect and learning, and are more resilient in the face of stressful conditions and external pressures. When these front-line staff are part of the team leading change, they can help shape the way change happens. They usually know better than anyone else why something will not work, and what it would take to make it work better. Their insights and perspectives are essential.

When organizations or systems try to make change to improve quality, they can make two common mistakes. One is to focus on changing individual behavior without including the context and systems in which the individuals work. Researchers are finding more and more that professional development has limited impact when it is disconnected from other change efforts or the everyday contexts in which educators work (Darling-Hammond, Wei, Andree, Richardson, & Orphanos, 2009; Douglass & Klerman, 2012). The second common mistake is to bring in outside experts to direct the change, without ensuring that teachers are co-creators in that change. For example, in the K–12 sector, which has been the focus of school reform efforts for far longer than the ECE sector, the dominant approach to school improvement for many years was to apply external standards and policy mandates in the form of prescribed curriculum, assessments, and accountability measures. Much of the professional autonomy that once characterized K–12 education was taken away and replaced with measures of teachers' fidelity in implementing a mandated, prescribed curriculum. Rather than acting as the designers and owners of the curriculum, teachers were treated as passive recipients. They were expected to adopt and implement, exactly as prescribed in the curriculum manual.

While these reforms likely offered some benefits associated with having a standardized curriculum, they often failed to result in the desired improvements in student outcomes. Schools often found that the changes did not take hold, and if they did, they were not sustained over time. Anthony Bryk, president of the Carnegie Foundation for the Advancement of Teaching, has been vocal about this problem. He and his colleagues at Carnegie and UCLA write, "Far too many efforts at improvement are designs delivered *to* educators rather than developed *with* them. Not surprisingly, then, when teachers are presented with new ideas for change, they may just mutter, 'This, too, shall pass'" (Bryk et al., 2015, p. 34, emphasis in original).

The K–12 school improvement literature affirms the importance of teacher leadership (Lieberman et al., 2017). One reason that co-creating improvement matters so much relates to what improvement scientists call variation. Variation means that one size does not fit all (Langley et al., 2009). Implementing new practices requires professional judgment and adaptation. Every child does not respond to a particular curriculum or lesson in the same way. We want improvement for all the children we teach, but when we implement a curriculum with fidelity to a prescribed model, we sometimes are expected to ignore the context and the variability that is inherent in real-world settings. A tested curriculum may be proven to work with one set of children in one context, but that does not ensure that it will result in those same benefits for every teacher in every school with all groups of children.

Variation is present in all human systems like classrooms, schools, and ECE programs (Bryk et al., 2015). That means that the way we teach must be driven not just by evidence-based practices, but also by practice-based evidence, the knowledge that teachers and other practitioners develop when they adapt, refine, and test strategies for getting good results with every child, knowing that children's development and learning vary widely. "Learning how to make interventions work effectively in the hands of different individuals in varied contexts is the problem to solve" (Bryk et al., 2015, p. 181). Improvement science offers tested methods that enable educators to test and adapt new practices, based on what actually works in their classrooms and programs with the children and families they serve.

Teachers' expertise and insights must inform the delivery of classroom teaching and their implementation of new practices. K–12 education has already begun to draw on the science of improvement. Attention is shifting to more collaborative professional approaches that recognize that change cannot be driven solely by top-down mandates. Improvement science offers key insights about how to effect change.

So how can we create and spread this kind of professional culture in our organizations and systems to respect and engage educators' expertise and leadership? One way is to adopt professional development and quality improvement processes that are designed specifically to elevate the role of teachers or other front-line or direct service staff. Next, I describe one such model, the Breakthrough Series Collaborative, and present the lessons learned from a study of one of its first applications in the ECE sector.

Key Insights About How to Effect Change Drawn from Improvement Science

- Ensure that the drivers of change are those who know the work best and are closest to the work.
- Focus more on action, avoiding the tendency to get stuck in the planning stage.
- Buy-in matters at all levels and depends on champions in many places.
- Be intentional about building positive relationships and mutual respect, in order to foster a culture of learning.
- Continually use data to inform and guide improvement.
- Foster peer accountability and collaborative problem solving.

THE BREAKTHROUGH SERIES COLLABORATIVE MODEL

The Breakthrough Series Collaborative (BSC) is a method for learning how to make improvements. It was designed to bridge the gap between knowledge and practice by creating a structure in which teams and organizations can learn from one another in order to create lasting improvement (Institute for Healthcare Improvement, 2003). The term *breakthrough* is important. A breakthrough happens when we overcome a barrier, surpass obstacles, and achieve a success that dramatically alters the outcomes we care about. When we achieve a breakthrough, we are making a discovery. Collaborative learning is at the heart of this model.

In the healthcare field, BSCs have achieved many successes, including some dramatic outcomes, such as reducing patient waiting times by 50%, reducing worker absenteeism by 25%, reducing ICU costs by 25%, and reducing hospitalizations for patients with congestive heart failure by 50% (Institute for Healthcare Improvement, 2003). Because of these successes, the BSC model has been used widely as a method for quality improvement (Arbour et al., 2016; Bailie, Si, O Donoghue, & Dowden, 2007; Institute for Healthcare Improvement, 2003; Kilo, 1998; O'Neill et al., 2011).

The BSC method is rooted in the belief that every system is perfectly designed to achieve the results it gets. That means that if we want to achieve different, or better, results, we must change not just individual practice, but the way the system works as a whole. The BSC model recognizes that not all changes lead to improvement. What worked somewhere else, with some other children, may not work everywhere, with every child. Therefore, it is necessary for educators to test and adapt their practice to find what works, for each and every child. The BSC model focuses on the use of data to determine the best strategies to achieve targeted outcomes in local contexts and then to promote the spread and sustainability of these improvements. Next these successes can be spread throughout the organization. At the heart of the BSC methodology is shared and collaborative leadership for change. A BSC brings together teams from within ECE programs to engage in collaborative learning and improvement designed to support the transfer of learning to practice, thereby closing the persistent gap between what we know and what we do.

WHAT HAPPENS IN A BSC?

Because a BSC involves bringing together multiple ECE programs, an organizing body typically coordinates the overall process. This body can be a professional association or committee, or some other group. It first identifies the area or topic that will be the focus for improvement, usually one where there is an identified need and a desire to make improvements, and one that is responsive to, and shaped by, the needs of those who want to participate. Often, it is an area of practice that has proven difficult to change. For example, in an ECE context, this might be something like reducing challenging behaviors in the classroom or engaging parents as partners. The organizing group collaborates with various stakeholders and partners to create a clear purpose about the desired outcome and the practices or changes that will result. This typically encompasses the research-informed practices that the group wants to target, as well as the workplace and contextual conditions that are necessary for supporting these practices.

An important part of this planning is to bring together diverse stakeholders and to include their insights about what it takes to make improvements in the selected area. These stakeholders include teachers, administrators, support staff, training and technical assistance providers, parents, and other key stakeholders. Through highly interactive activities, the meeting enables participants to provide concrete and specific input into and refine the plan for change; this process often is called the change framework. It serves to engage people early on in the BSC and can help develop a cadre of champions at various levels. Then the planning team recruits a group of "faculty" who possess diverse expertise related to the selected focus area to help provide support to teams as they work to make change. The planning team and these faculty form a learning community that leads the BSC and supports the work of the participating early education programs.

Next, ECE programs interested in participating are recruited. Each program identifies a team of five to eight members that includes a mix of teachers, parents, support staff, and administrators and program leaders. The composition of these teams is a core feature of this model. By bringing together participants from across diverse roles in an ECE program, the BSC fosters a collaborative learning community within the organization. In contrast to traditional professional development approaches, where one teacher might have training or coaching on a specific topic, here many individuals learn together as a group. They plan together how to make changes in their practice and overcome common barriers to change. Many ECE teachers work in teams, and planning, coordination, and collaboration are essential if change is to happen and be sustained in their classrooms and programs. The team composition also ensures that formal leadership in the organization is engaged and able to put into place the supports teachers need in order to make change.

The BSC organizing group engages these participating teams in a series of activities to orient and prepare them for the process. The goal here is to clarify roles, responsibilities, expectations, and processes. During this phase, participants receive specific guidance and step-by-step tools to assist in team-building; they learn foundational content about the changes, data and measurement, project management, and center-wide buy-in and communication.

After this prework phase, teams move into the action period. During this time, they all meet together three to four times for day-long learning sessions, where teams share ideas and learn about how to test change ideas, use data, and spread effective new practices throughout the organization. At these sessions, teams participate in several kinds of learning. This process can include training on evidence-based practices related to the area of focus; it also can include coaching with teams about how to apply the Plan, Do, Study, Act (PDSA) process to test and spread changes. After each learning session, team members put new ideas into action at their organization, using that process. PDSAs are cycles of planning, doing, studying, and acting (Langley et al., 2009). Members of a team plan a change, implement it, measure its success, and revise it to test again or begin to spread successful changes.

The changes start out small, perhaps occurring with one person, classroom, or branch, and if successful, they grow into systemic change. The PDSA process becomes a tool that can enable teachers and other staff to adapt and modify their changes. One teacher I interviewed explained how transformative the PDSA tool had been for her. She said that she had learned how to keep trying with a challenging child in her class even when one strategy had failed to work. Rather than give up, or blame the child for not responding well to her approach, she just kept developing new ideas with her team and trying them, measuring them until she found one that worked for that child.

An essential aspect of a BSC is the use of monthly metrics. These metrics are measures of the kinds of outcomes teams are trying to achieve, and they enable teams to reflect on these data and learn from their progress (Douglass, 2016b; Doyle, Agosti, Rivers, & Douglass, 2016). For example, one metric might be the frequency and quality of parent–teacher communications. By tracking this, team members are able to identify patterns, strengths, and gaps in this communication, and test strategies to see how they influence the metric and help teams achieve improvements. Through the use of a collaborative website, monthly calls, and learning sessions, teams can learn and grow from one another in a shared learning environment (Mallon, Agosti, & Dougherty, 2004). This helps spread what is working in organizations to an even larger audience. Teams are supported to learn and grow from their peers' successes and struggles, encouraging the growth of the field as a whole. By the end of a BSC, the goal is to build capacity within teams and organizations to continue to create and sustain improvement.

THREE FOUNDATIONAL IDEAS

Throughout the BSC process, three foundational ideas are taught, modeled, and reinforced. First, anyone can test ideas in a BSC: All team members contribute and test ideas, whether they are the director, a teacher, or a parent. The BSC cultivates mutual respect for the ideas, insights, and perspectives of each member. Second, consensus is not needed. Most planning processes require consensus before change can be implemented. Consensus is often a lengthy process and can stifle the creativity and number of ideas generated (Mallon, Agosti, & Dougherty, 2004). Jen Agosti, a BSC consultant and colleague of mine, has led more than 30 collaboratives in health, child welfare, and now ECE settings. She often talks about how skilled we are when it comes to talking ourselves *out* of doing something. Someone has an idea and brings it to a meeting. At the meeting, people quickly move to identifying all the reasons that idea might not work. By the end of the meeting, the idea is dead in the water. The BSC model is designed to interrupt this tendency to get so caught up in planning that no one actually is trying anything new. It encourages the rapid testing of ideas, utilizing the philosophy that the more ideas, the better. A new idea is tested only on the smallest possible scale, with something that can be done often within the week. Then the conversations move to learning from testing ideas, refining or identifying other ideas, and always measuring whether those ideas get results closer to the desired outcomes. The goal of the BSC is to test changes and let the results speak for themselves, creating consensus in the long run. The third foundational idea is that learning to improve is inherently a collaborative process. Therefore, the BSC emphasizes the sharing of ideas, both within and across teams, to promote peer learning and build an ongoing, sustainable learning community.

To do all this requires relationships of mutual respect and the presence of what is called psychological safety, an individual's perceptions of the consequences and benefits of taking interpersonal risks in a particular context, such as the workplace (Edmondson & Lei, 2014). Psychological safety in the workplace means that employees feel comfortable expressing their thoughts, ideas, and concerns; they do not fear belittlement or retaliation. A review of the literature on psychological safety highlights the need of employees to feel safe in order to learn, contribute, and perform effectively in the workplace (Edmondson, 1999; Edmondson & Lei, 2014; Nembhard & Edmondson, 2012). Organizational research has identified psychological safety as a critical factor in individual voice, teamwork, team learning, and organizational learning.

Research shows that when employees do not feel psychologically safe in the workplace, they are far less likely to speak up, share ideas, try new strategies, or voice a concern. Psychological safety is therefore especially important when it comes to making change. Furthermore, not feeling safe leads employees to an increased likelihood of burnout and job turnover (Dollard & Bakker, 2010; Sprang, Craig, & Clark, 2011). Creating work relationships that are supportive and empowering is essential in working effectively in teams (Bradley, Postlethwaite, Klotz, Hamdani, & Brown, 2012; Coles,

Dartnall, & Astbury, 2013). The BSC is designed to foster meetings, organizations, and learning collaboratives as a whole that are safe, reflective, and participatory. This helps establish an organizational culture of learning.

THE BSC ON TRAUMA-INFORMED ECE

I studied the use of the BSC methodology in a project in urban ECE programs. This project was designed to promote the adoption of trauma-informed practices in six ECE programs serving children from birth to age 5 in low-income families living in communities experiencing high levels of violence and trauma (Douglass, 2016b, 2016d; Doyle et al., 2016). Each participating ECE program formed a team of six people, including a senior administrator, a program director, two teachers, an early childhood mental health consultant, and a parent. They brought expertise in areas such as parenting, ECE program administration, mental health, and trauma. Faculty provided training, coaching, and consultation to support the ECE teams.

Working together over an 18-month period, these teams learned about the impact of trauma and evidence-informed strategies for supporting children and families, and they developed and tested practical, sustainable strategies for implementing trauma-informed practice. They participated in collective, improvement-oriented supports, such as monthly conference calls, quarterly 2-day learning sessions, collecting and using monthly improvement metrics, team coaching and technical assistance, and biweekly team meetings. This BSC was led by a multidisciplinary organizing group with members from public health, ECE, child welfare, and early childhood mental health.

The study focused on how this BSC influenced the organizations' efforts to make and sustain change. I wanted to understand how early educators in particular learned and then implemented new practices as a result of participating in this type of professional development model. We found that the BSC helped build an organizational infrastructure to support teacher and parent leadership, which in turn resulted in improvement of trauma-informed practices.

The Power of Cross-Role Team Meetings

One of the most transformative strategies used in this project was to establish a regular, weekly team meeting, composed of people who had different roles—administrators, teachers, parents, support staff. Rather than just sending in a coach to work individually with teachers, or a consultant to work with the director, the BSC engaged a team of people from across different levels and roles within each organization to lead the change. In most of the participating programs, teachers had been assigned to work directly with children all day, with no paid planning time; they had no regular time to communicate with an early childhood mental health consultant or with teachers in the other classrooms. A key task early on in the BSC was, therefore, to overcome the barriers to establishing a weekly team meeting routine.

These meetings deeply affected the educators, the teams, and the organizations involved. Teachers reported feeling empowered and more respected by their peers and supervisors. Teachers—and parents, too—became agents for change. One teacher explained, "I've become a stronger teacher; I'm known more in the community. It's let me spread my wings, and it's made me feel strong and that I deserve the same respect as all involved in this." These teams started to see how valuable the educators' perspectives were and how this filled a gap in the change process where they worked. That gave many educators the courage to take action and risks they previously would not have considered: Teams made changes that otherwise would not have been possible.

But it wasn't just having these meetings; it was the quality of the meetings. When someone threw out an idea, no one else would say, "That's the worst idea I've ever heard," or "We tried that last year and it didn't work." The meetings were designed to offer a psychologically safe space—a relational space—where everyone could speak up, think creatively, try out possible solutions, and voice their ideas. No ideas were assumed to be wrong or bad. Because of this climate of mutual respect, people came to see and value how their work fit together with the work of others on their team.

The teams got amazing results. One had focused on improving regular, two-way communication with parents. An educator from this team described a success she'd had with a parent she'd been struggling to connect with: "When I saw [that parent], I shed a tear because, at the beginning of the year, this was a woman who was dropping F-bombs, who wouldn't come to the school, who wouldn't pick up phone calls, who wouldn't return letters. And at the end of the school year, now she's showing up for everything; she's sending me notes and giving me phone calls just to check in on her daughter."

These team meetings really worked in these early childhood programs, but the work was not easy, particularly in organizations where staff were working directly with children and families all day long. It took these teams a lot of time to figure out how to schedule their meetings. Once they saw it was possible, they reaped powerful benefits, and they sustained the use of this meeting structure even beyond the formal end of the BSC.

The study found that the BSC had strengthened the leadership of both teachers and parents, showing that a team structure can strengthen the leadership of parents and transform an organization's capacity to deliver family-centered care. Daniela, a mother who became part of a change team on a similar project, had emigrated to Boston from Honduras and had been a single mother since her husband was deported, just 1 month after their son's birth. Her experience on the team was transformational. She explained, "For me, being a parent-leader means having a voice. It means belonging. It means feeling empowered. Having a family—you know what I mean? And it means being a part of a driving force for a good change."

Her transformation as a leader taught her a lot about herself and what she could accomplish. "What did I learn about myself? That I was stronger than I imagined. And it was from being respected, being seen as a leader, for having my voice heard." Just as the educators on the teams came to see themselves—and to be seen—as leaders, so did parents, all as a result of being a member of a team.

This meeting structure, with safety for speaking up and having a voice, helps utilize the expertise of direct service staff and families, with all individuals having equal standing. This can elevate leadership at all levels, enabling teams to coordinate and strengthen their work with children and families.

Learning to Test Change

Teachers frequently reported feeling empowered by their role in the improvement process. In this study, teachers were engaged in learning the quality improvement process using PDSA cycles, the structured inquiry protocol for testing, studying, adapting, and spreading improvements. This protocol was brand-new to the early childhood teams in this project. Learning to approach problems of practice and improvement in this way was not easy, but it proved to be transformative to many of these teams. One teacher explained how learning to use this protocol shifted how she approached her work to engage families. She learned how to customize her engagement strategies, to find what worked for each family, rather than expecting all families to respond to the same approach. She explained:

> In the beginning, I was trying to communicate with this parent. I offered to do her child's progress report over the phone. So I felt like I was taking the steps and she was brushing it off. Through the PDSAs, I learned, "OK that didn't work, so what am I going to do next to try to communicate with that parent?" rather than just, "That didn't work; I'll just back off." And that's when the PDSA of trying a new idea came to mind. My parent approach has changed. Now I'm persistent in a way that's respectful. I just have to keep trying to find another way if something doesn't work.

She made a transformative shift in how she approached her work with families. Rather than give up when a family did not respond to her efforts to engage, rather than assume that the family did not want to engage, she now had a flexible protocol, which helped her try different approaches until she found one that worked for each family. This protocol helped her to be curious, not discouraged or blaming, when it came to the challenges she faced with families.

Many teachers described how empowering it was to see that even small changes could have a big impact. They learned this through their own testing of small changes, and by using data to measure the impact of the changes. In a similar study I conducted of an initiative to improve family-engagement practices, teachers from one program were talking about a new practice that was working and sticking (Douglass & Klerman, 2012). They had realized that when children were being dropped off in the morning, teachers would greet the children by name, but not the parents. One teacher even said to me, "I didn't even know my parents' names." The teachers came up with an idea to test: They modified the attendance sheets that sat at the entry to the classroom to include the parents' names next to each child's name. They predicted that this would help them learn the parents' names quickly, and they could then greet parents by name each day—which might make parents feel more respected and valued.

The teachers observed a transformative impact of using parents' names. They built relationships with parents they had never talked with before. One of these teachers told me:

> One of the things I've learned is sometimes we don't need to think so big. We try to overwhelm ourselves thinking about all these big changes but if we did 10 small things we would have a greater impact with families. I know it seems so minute that somebody would be like, "Oh for goodness' sake, because you said hi to everybody you think you would make a difference." But you know, if you were standing in that spot, you'd have seen that it made a difference.

Empowering the Leadership Within

The BSC strengthened organizations' capacity for change, in part by building positive, respectful, and reciprocal relationships throughout the organization. The ECE programs that participated in the BSC built a learning culture. The relationships we establish with one another in the workplace carry over to the work we do with children and families. Relational organizations know this. If we are to improve what we do with children and families, we must simultaneously improve the supportive nature of the organizations where educators work. Relational organizations have structures that nurture, develop, and sustain positive relationships. They use structures like cross-role teams to elevate the expertise from all levels. In this BSC, all of this supported teachers as change agents, able to implement new practices in ways that became part of their daily routines.

This enabled the teachers to speak up about the stresses they encountered in their work that sometimes were a barrier to improvement. All the programs involved in this BSC served a high percentage of children who had been exposed to trauma. Educators' secondary exposure to trauma can have an impact on them, but none of these ECE programs had put systems into place to support educators. This became a focus in the BSC. Secondary, or vicarious, trauma is the experience of symptoms of trauma as a result of empathetic engagement with others' trauma. Such experiences can deeply affect teachers and influence their worldview and self-concept. Those in human service fields, like ECE, are more likely to experience secondary trauma then employees in other environments (Newell & MacNeil, 2010).

A professional culture that supports and values "caring for the carer" is essential for those who provide safe and quality care to others (Coles et al., 2013). Working with trauma victims affects people in various ways. Early educators may have their own experiences of trauma as well, on top of working with children and families exposed to trauma. Thus, it is important for the workplace to pay particular attention to developing a supportive work environment, one that reduces stress and builds resilience.

The science is clear: People do not change the way they interact with children or families because someone tells them to. They make change because they come to see themselves, and others, as leaders, as people with valuable expertise and insights. They make change because the environments in which they work become more supportive and facilitative of change. In relational organizations, formal leaders actively learn about and draw upon the unique talents and strengths of the members of the organization. Rather than focusing on what people cannot do, relational organizations focus on what people *can* do—and connect with those strengths.

That is the power of creating a collaborative culture of learning and improvement. It can cultivate the expertise and leadership within to lead change, in smarter, more informed, and more sustainable ways. A program administrator who found himself transformed by the leadership that developed among parents like Daniela explained, "We began to see parents as people with their own expertise. Because they knew exactly how to run things, what things work, and what did not work. That really changed the tone of the conversation. We started looking at parents more as leaders, rather than the people that we serve." His words speak to the urgent need and transformative potential to unleash the leadership from within our organizations as we seek to deliver quality care and education for children and their families. What if we all started looking at parents and the people working in our organizations more as leaders?

CONCLUSION

As noted at the beginning of this chapter, efforts to improve quality can be designed in ways to cultivate educator leadership or not. Most of what we do now in ECE minimizes the opportunity for early educators to be leaders and active agents of change. All too often, educators are seen as passive adopters of change, rather than architects and co-creators of it. The science of improvement explains why it is so important to engage the leadership of those who work most closely with children and families.

This chapter illustrates another way that professional development and quality improvement approaches can cultivate the leadership of early educators as architects and leaders of change. The BSC methodology offers a concrete strategy for doing just that. It shows us what this looks like and how it contrasts with more traditional approaches in our field.

Part III

A LEADERSHIP DEVELOPMENT ECOSYSTEM: CULTIVATING THE LEADERSHIP WE NEED

CHAPTER 8

What Is a Leadership Development Ecosystem and Why Do We Need One?

What if we believed that early educators could drive change to improve ECE? What would we do differently? I propose that we would redesign our approach to professional development and quality improvement. We would create a leadership development ecosystem that respects the expertise of early educators and supports their active engagement in change in a systemic and ongoing way. We would create an environment that enables, cultivates, and benefits from diverse leadership. This chapter defines a leadership development ecosystem and describes how it can advance and further professionalize our field.

EARLY EDUCATORS CO-CREATING A VISION FOR AN ECOSYSTEM

We launched the early educator leadership development program at UMass Boston in 2012 with the goal of enhancing educators' capacity to be active agents of change. They learned how to apply their unique expertise as educators to solving the problems they faced in their practice. The program's success exceeded my wildest dreams—by the time they completed the program, educators reported gaining a new sense of themselves as leaders, gaining confidence in their potential to be agents of change, and feeling empowered and clear on their purpose as leaders—what they wanted to improve and how to get started. These graduates have done incredible work already. Their leadership has inspired me and so many others.

However, we soon learned there was more work to do to support leadership in more sustained and systemic ways. These leaders were passionate about their ideas for change. They had a vision for what they wanted to change, which often required doing something new and different to address a persistent problem or challenge. However, about a year after completing the program, some of these educators started to feel frustrated and isolated. They were facing roadblocks. Some told me that their bosses or coworkers weren't on the same page about the change they were trying to make. One educator told me, "The world wasn't ready for my ideas." Many found they lacked the financial resources or connections to the right people to advance their change plan.

I learned from these educators. It takes more than a leadership program to support and sustain leadership for change. I came to realize how few supports there are out there in our field for the entrepreneurial, innovative, purpose-driven leadership of early educators. There aren't many leadership development programs in ECE in the first place. Then, once someone completes the training, our field lacks ongoing systems to support and nurture this leadership. In addition, many of our professional development opportunities are not designed to engage educators as co-creators of change and improvement. Too often, these systems and policies are set up to do just the opposite, seeing incapacity rather than capacity in our workforce. We need to build a leadership and innovation ecosystem in our field to nurture and sustain early educator leaders and to more fully catalyze action for innovation and change in an ongoing way.

WHAT IS A LEADERSHIP DEVELOPMENT ECOSYSTEM?

What is an ecosystem? In nature, an ecosystem refers to a community of organisms that interact with one another in a living system. This same concept, of nested systems that interact in reciprocal ways, has been applied to human contexts as well. Bronfenbrenner's ecological systems theory explains how a child's development is influenced by the world around him/her (Bronfenbrenner, 1979; Bronfenbrenner & Morris, 1998). Bronfenbrenner talks about multiple levels of an ecosystem that impact a child's development and learning. The "microsystem" is the most direct level of influence and includes the child's home and school environments, relationships, and interactions. The second level is the "mesosystem," which refers to the things that interact with the microsystem and have an indirect impact on children. These include things like the relationship between the child's parents and his/her teacher. The "exosystem" consists of the factors beyond the child's immediate environment, such as parental life issues and work, and the community and neighborhood. The "macrosystem" is made up of the cultural, economic, and political environments surrounding a child. In order to understand a child's development, we must understand the systems in which the child's growth occurs.

We can apply this human ecology framework to educators and their professional growth and learning. Just as in other human systems, early educators perform their work in the context of multiple influencing contexts, environments, and relationships. They develop as professionals and as leaders in this way, too. The innovation sector frequently draws upon ecosystems frameworks. In order to encourage innovation, what needs to be in place at each level of the ecosystem in which emerging innovators work? These innovation ecosystems frequently consist of entrepreneurial leadership training, access to finance and mentoring networks, innovation incubators, and a policy and regulatory context that support and promote all of this (Cameron, 2012; Hamer, 2010; Mulgan, 2006; Smith & Petersen, 2006; United Nations Conference on Trade and Development, 2011). A leadership development ecosystem is similar, consisting of the supports, resources, and policies needed to systematically nurture the development of leadership in the ECE sector.

WHY DO WE NEED A LEADERSHIP DEVELOPMENT ECOSYSTEM?

In the absence of a supportive leadership development system, we are wasting our richest resource—the diverse talent within our field. So many experienced and passionate early educators leave each year because they lack opportunities to continue to grow and thrive in this profession. As the UMass Boston leadership graduates taught me, the field lacks the supports educators need to continue to develop as leaders and as change agents.

We need an ecosystem, not just stand-alone leadership development programs. The traditional understanding of a leadership development pathway relies on a sequence of linear steps to a formal leadership position in organizations or systems. Someone desiring a formal leadership position could participate in training, build a network, and move into a leadership position. However, as has been argued here, leadership is much more than a formal position. Leadership happens at all levels of an organization or a profession, and transformative change requires this collective engagement.

When leadership is defined as a relational process of influencing change—which does not require a formal position—the concept of a leadership pathway must expand. Rather than a predefined sequence of steps leading to a formal leadership position, a leadership pathway becomes a more emergent process of driving change in the context of the work/professional setting. Such a pathway requires more than just a one-time leadership development experience, and instead requires an ecosystem within the field (locally and more broadly) that offers ongoing supports and resources for this leadership to thrive.

An early educator leadership ecosystem also offers greater possibilities for building inclusive and diverse leadership within the field. Preserving and promoting racial, cultural, and linguistic diversity needs to be an explicit priority in a leadership development ecosystem (Kagan & Bowman, 1997;

Whitebook, Kipnis, & Bellm, 2008). ECE has the most racially and linguistically diverse teaching workforce in the entire education sector. The diversity within the ECE workforce is strong at the level of the teaching ranks, and engaging and supporting the leadership development of educators is one way to strengthen the inclusiveness of leadership pathways in the field.

This workforce diversity is an asset that other education sectors have been struggling to attain. For example, the nonprofit group Education Pioneers released an important report on increasing leadership diversity in K–12 education (Education Pioneers & Koya Leadership Partners, 2014). Their survey of educational institutions found a gap between the intention to promote diversity and the actual actions taken in these institutions. They developed an organizational audit checklist for assessing diversity practices in educational institutions.

Diverse leadership has a multitude of documented benefits, particularly when it comes to improvement and innovation (Janus, 2016; Kagan & Bowman, 1997; Ospina & Foldy, 2010). For example, research shows better results for problem solving and innovation when those with diverse perspectives and viewpoints and varied backgrounds work together to design solutions (Hewlett, Marshall, & Sherbin, 2013). The Stanford University design school refers to this as "radical collaboration." Diversity in leadership is also important in delivering effective and culturally responsive early care and education and family supports, with leaders who represent the rich cultural and linguistic backgrounds of the families and communities they serve. It is crucial to preserve and strengthen this diversity as we cultivate broad and inclusive leadership from within the field.

Supports for early educator leadership also must recognize that ECE is primarily a small business sector, made up of a large number of businesses owned and operated by women and minorities. Few of the ECE professional development and quality improvement resources and policies appear to recognize this fact or see the potential to drive improvement through enhancing the strength of these small businesses. Small business innovation has long been the foundation for growth and prosperity in the United States. Public- and private-sector entities cultivate a business-sector innovation ecosystem with tax incentives, workforce training resources, and targeted support programs for start-up enterprises in technology, healthcare, and other mainstream industries (Dempwolf, Auer, & D'Ippolito, 2014). Unfortunately, the infrastructure supporting socially directed enterprises such as ECE programs, primarily led by female entrepreneurs and often in disadvantaged communities, is weak to nonexistent. It is not surprising, therefore, that these businesses, so vital to the productivity and growth of the local economy, are struggling in both rural and urban communities.

The lack of support for ECE businesses is a lost opportunity to view this sector as a significant growth industry in our economy and a leading contributor to children's learning. The characterization of the delivery of child care as a social service or soft skill often obscures the need to create an environment that supports this as a sustainable enterprise—one that is essential to the success of all other industries because it ensures current workforce productivity and also nurtures and educates our future workforce.

Let me give an example from Boston, where I work. The ECE industry in Boston is a critical sector of the local economy, with approximately 200 licensed child-care centers and more than 400 licensed family child-care businesses. Consider this profile of just one of Boston's neighborhoods, the greater Roxbury community, where we work extensively with local educators and small business owners. Of Roxbury's 4,933 young children between the ages of 0 and 5, approximately half are served by 154 ECE businesses (consisting of 127 family, or home-based, child-care businesses and 27 center-based businesses). These businesses employ more than 500 people (teachers, assistant teachers, directors, and other staff), who are predominantly low-income women of color (Boston EQUIP, 2010). According to the 2010 U.S. Census, the unemployment rate in Roxbury is 16.5%, and 35% of households are living below the poverty line. Gentrification pressures impact the stability of local businesses; early care and education is no exception.

The success of these ECE businesses is central not only to the economic stability of the neighborhood, but also to closing the opportunity and achievement gap between children from low-income families and their peers from middle- and upper-income families. Yet the challenges of operating these businesses, without the support of an entrepreneurial ecosystem, often force these entrepreneurs to shutter their doors or to seek secondary jobs, public assistance, or loans to make ends meet. The lack of leadership development opportunities reduces the sector's capacity to achieve the level of quality that can transform child outcomes. In building and strengthening systems in ECE, we must directly challenge the marginalization of ECE in local economic development, urban planning, housing, and small business supports.

THE FOUNDATIONS FOR A LEADERSHIP DEVELOPMENT ECOSYSTEM

What kind of ecosystem is needed to develop, nurture, and sustain leadership for change within the diverse ECE workforce? The stories and studies I have presented in this book point to the kinds of opportunities, supports, and resources that are needed to cultivate leadership for change from all levels. Early educators who want to lead change can face many challenges in taking their big ideas out into the real world. The alumni from the UMass Boston leadership programs came together to envision a more supportive ecosystem. We convened 100 early educators and other stakeholders to envision and co-design a leadership ecosystem to put into place the supports educators need. They identified many of the same elements found in other fields. They proposed establishing a network of like-minded educators and leaders, mentors to help support and develop ideas and overcome barriers, and an innovation lab where early educators can get the support to test their ideas, refine them, and use them in the real world in ways that make a difference for children and families. And then they called for resources to make this leadership more visible—so everyone could see and understand the possibilities of early educators leading change and improvement.

We launched a new Institute for Early Education Leadership and Innovation at UMass Boston, to be the home for building and testing a model for this new ecosystem. We began to study how other sectors build systems to nurture this kind of leadership. In doing this, I have talked with so many generous individuals and groups from within and far beyond the ECE field. They have shared insights and lessons learned from successes and failures of similar efforts in the healthcare, K–12 education, higher education, and community service sectors.

One insight I have taken away from all of this is that believing in the possibility of early educator leadership is at the heart of this ecosystem. Peter Senge, an organizational scholar from MIT, is known across the world for his groundbreaking work on learning organizations and leadership. He writes about an "ecology of leadership," in which organizations create the conditions that support leadership from the front lines of direct service, as well as middle managerial and executive leadership (Senge, 2006, p. 319). But what does it take to make this kind of shift, to build this kind of ecology for leadership within organizations, systems, and our field? As Senge writes: "At its heart, the traditional view of leadership is based on assumptions of people's powerlessness, their lack of personal vision and inability to master the forces of change, deficits which can be remedied only by a few great leaders" (p. 321). I have encountered these very beliefs about the ECE workforce, rooted in a tendency to see deficits more than strengths.

Building a leadership development ecosystem, therefore, must go hand in hand with efforts to overcome assumptions that early educators cannot or do not want to co-create and lead improvement, innovation, and transformation. As I have argued in earlier chapters, elevating the visibility of early educator leadership is a powerful and transformative act, and we must do more of it. We must cultivate the strengths-based and relational systems thinking that foster an ecology for early educator leadership.

CONCLUSION

This chapter opened with a question. What if we believed that early educators could be active agents of change to improve ECE? What would we do differently? Decades of research on change and quality improvement confirm the essential importance of a relational and systems approach. This approach differs dramatically from the status quo. The science behind the relational and systems approach provides concrete guidance for designing this ecosystem. What that means is that in order to do things differently, or in a new way, we will need to build an ecosystem capable of nourishing the kind of leadership we need to advance.

CHAPTER 9

Building the Leadership Development Ecosystem

A leadership development ecosystem can create the environment we need in order to nurture the innovative, entrepreneurial, and skilled leadership of early educators. This book has presented the research and theoretical foundations for supporting early educators as the active agents for change in our field. When we cultivate and support the leadership of early educators, we can make change in smarter, more informed, and more sustainable ways. Earlier I described why an ecosystem model is a helpful framework for thinking about how to build an ECE leadership development system. An ecosystem recognizes that each part of a system is highly interdependent with the other parts (Bronfenbrenner & Morris, 1998). Early educators work and grow professionally in the context of multiple influencing contexts, environments, and relationships. An ecological systems framework helps us think about each of those contexts and how we might shape them to better support professional and leadership development.

How can we infuse the ecosystem in which early educators work with the supportive environments, experiences, and resources that enable them to grow and thrive as agents of change?

COMPONENTS OF THE LEADERSHIP DEVELOPMENT ECOSYSTEM

A leadership development ecosystem in ECE must include supports and resources at all levels. Much of this book has highlighted strategies for developing the leadership capacity of individuals and of organizations. An ecosystem puts these and other strategies into place at multiple levels, to create an environment that supports and continually sustains leaders (see Figure 9.1). This chapter describes the key components of this ecosystem.

Supportive Workplaces

The most direct influences on leadership development are found closest to educators. Educators need a supportive workplace that recognizes their

Figure 9.1. ECE Leadership Development Ecosystem

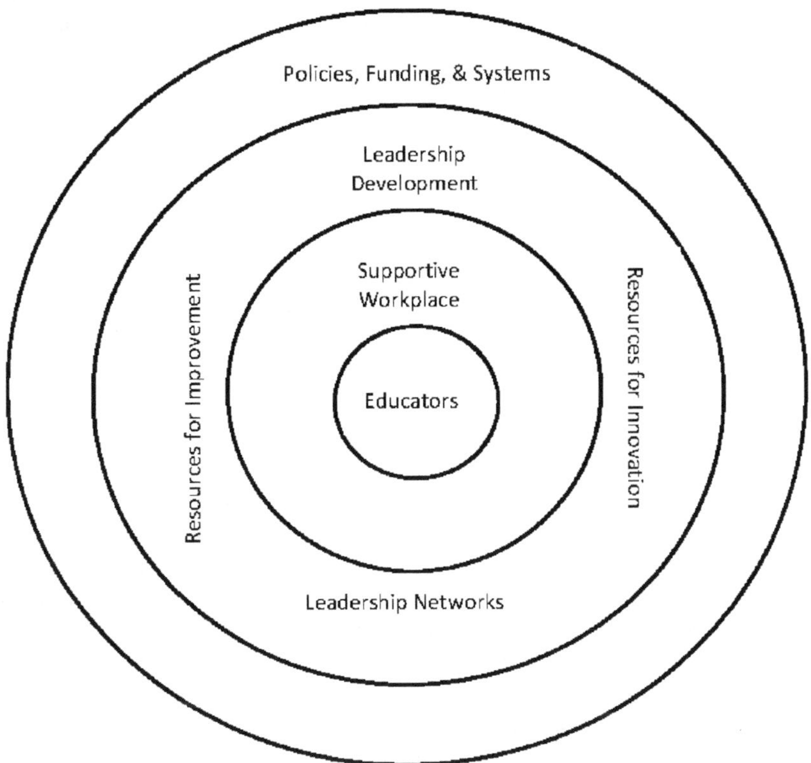

potential, creates opportunities to lead, and cultivates a culture of continuous learning. I often hear from educators that the biggest obstacle they faced in improving their practices was their executive director or coworkers, or other workplace challenges. Some were fortunate to have had wonderfully supportive directors who were able to appreciate and advocate for the leadership ideas of educators. Others worked for administrators who wanted to decide what needed to be changed and how, or were unfamiliar with or threatened by the practices educators were trying to implement. Coworkers sometimes got in the way, telling them that the idea had been tried before and did not work. Family child-care providers often work in isolation, which presents different kinds of challenges. They too benefit from supportive networks and professional relationships, in a broader "workplace" context or their professional networks.

Of course, there is a reason and a context for these workplace barriers, and directors who must manage multiple demands and priorities, often with inadequate resources, face difficult realities. Many who work in child-care centers have no paid planning time when teachers, administrators, and/or specialists can meet. Educators need time during the work day to problem-solve and to be inspired by one another and generate creative solutions that they then can put to the test and in many cases retest as they make adjustments. As with most creative work, there should be an atmosphere of trial and error to discover the best approach. They need an organizational culture of learning, enabled by respectful relationships and supportive structures and policies that foster shared leadership. Without this, the result is too often a shutting-down of the creativity, innovation, and problem-solving passions of teachers, preventing the possibility of developing a culture of learning and improvement that benefits everyone. Supporting the capacity of ECE programs to be hospitable environments for creativity, and to embody a culture of learning, is essential. As organizational leaders, directors need more support about how to cultivate these learning environments that we know make a difference.

We can maximize educators' leadership impact within the context of the ECE programs and systems where they work, by helping ECE programs build their capacity for improvement and innovation. This points to the importance of an ecosystem that builds organizational capacity for improvement and learning. One of the biggest challenges ECE programs face today, when it comes to organizational change and quality improvement, is the dearth of resources. Almost all efforts to improve ECE quality focus on individuals—changing individual teachers' behaviors or working with a director alone rather than engaging teams from organizations. As a result, the field is not well equipped to create learning organizations.

Promising models that already exist can be embedded or adapted for this ecosystem. For example, models such as the Breakthrough Series Collaborative create collaborative networks among ECE programs to support improvement and leadership. The BSC model's home is the Institute for Healthcare Improvement, which offers a wide range of organizational improvement and front-line leadership training and resources for the health sector. Higher education institutions play an important role in co-designing these kinds of supports. For over 2 decades, the McCormick Center for Early Childhood Leadership at National Louis University has been developing a rich toolkit of resources for early childhood administrators and directors to drive organizational change. The Relational Coordination Research Collaborative is another entity that connects organizations across many sectors with the kinds of resources and strategies needed in order to build resilient and high-performing learning organizations, capable of cultivating leadership for innovation and change.

Including these networks and resources in an ecosystem can enable us to build and strengthen local early childhood program hubs of innovation and excellence. This fosters an enabling environment for innovation and quality improvement through these organizational systems interventions, which enhance coordination, relational leadership, and co-creation, and foster a culture of inquiry. ECE programs must be connected to the ecosystem that provides the tools and resources they need to create hospitable conditions for the engaged leadership of early educators. As Senge (2006) argues, "Without effective local line leaders, new ideas—no matter how compelling—do not get translated into action, and the intentions behind change initiatives from the top can easily be thwarted" (p. 319). ECE must build its capacity to support organizations that effectively engage the leadership of educators and create a culture of learning and positive workplace relationships and climate. To do so will require a new approach that reflects the paradigm shift from the current focus on individuals and compliance, to one focused on systems thinking and learning.

Leadership Development Programs

Professional development services and programming are the next level of influence in the ecosystem. Currently, most professional development in ECE focuses on basic entry-level knowledge and skills, with few more advanced offerings. This is where we need to expand leadership development in two important ways. First, all early educators should have access to leadership development opportunities, and opportunities for experienced educators must be greatly expanded. Second, the scope and content of leadership development should not be limited only to the skills and competencies needed for management or formal leadership positions.

I have found that experienced and committed early educators are hungry for knowledge and skills for designing and testing innovations in their practice in classrooms and family child-care programs. We have begun to form affinity groups or cohorts of educators who share a focus for their leadership. These groups focus on important areas for improvement.

These educators have ideas, big and small, and want the support to grow and implement these ideas. So many educators have innovative

Important Areas for ECE Improvement

- Early STEM learning
- Social and emotional learning
- Early childhood special education
- Family engagement
- Policy and advocacy
- Workforce compensation and benefits
- Family child care and ECE small business model innovations

and creative ideas for change, for doing things in a new or different way. Entrepreneurial leadership training is still new to ECE, but fills an important gap when it comes to building capacity to tap the expertise and insights of those who know the most about teaching and caring for young children in ECE settings.

Leadership development programs can operate in many ways. Higher education can play an important role at this level of the ecosystem, too. For example, UMass Boston's early childhood academic programs now offer both undergraduate and graduate coursework on leadership and change, including entrepreneurial leadership, policy and advocacy, as well as the science of improvement, creativity and innovation, and systems thinking. Importantly, these programs are all designed for early educators who are currently in the workforce. These educators bring real-world problems and solutions and connect those in powerful ways with their academic learning. Higher education can build multiple pathways to this kind of entrepreneurial leadership training, for undergraduates, graduates, and practitioners in the field (preservice, early career, and advanced career pathways). State and local professional development systems also can offer similar leadership learning opportunities. The more these learning opportunities can be closely connected and even situated within ECE programs and settings, the more this will facilitate educators' capacity to implement new knowledge in their practice. ECE director training and credentialing in the field also must be expanded, so more educators and administrators have access. When it comes to training ECE directors and administrators, it is important to equip them with the skills needed for cultivating a culture of learning in their organizations.

Access to Resources and Networks

Sectors with robust innovation ecologies know that successful creative and entrepreneurial leaders need access to the resources that drive innovation: intellectual capital, human capital, and financial capital (Smith & Petersen, 2006). Intellectual capital is very much the kind of training described above, which educators need to be able to access from higher education institutions or other professional development systems. They need access to current science about early learning and child development, as well as about leadership, organizational change, and policy.

Human capital refers to the people and networks that an educator needs in order to develop, implement, and test an innovation. At our annual ECE Leadership Forum at UMass Boston, educators present their ideas and plans for change to a diverse audience of ECE stakeholders from across our state. They then engage in formal and informal dialogue designed to refine their thinking and connect with the people and information they need in order to implement their plans for improvement. They build the kinds of networks that can open doors. Sometimes this is a state agency staff person who offers to mentor an educator through a complicated state approval process for launching a new kind of ECE program. Other times, this is a philanthropic organization that offers to work with the educator to identify possible partnerships and funding opportunities. One toddler teacher who was a student of mine designed an innovative app to promote language development and parent–teacher partnerships through sharing of culturally relevant songs. To test her idea beyond her own classroom, she needed a mentor with technological expertise, and access to financing.

Financial capital refers to various kinds of funding that can support the development of ideas and the testing of innovations. Financial capital is a central component of the entrepreneurial ecosystem in other sectors and must be accessible at the local level and supported at the policy level as well. Few early educators can access such resources currently. The business and technology sectors take these resources for granted, and rightly so. They know they are essential for improvement. This should be no different in ECE. That is how our field will advance in smarter ways, driven by the insights of those closest to the work.

These supports enable entrepreneurial activity to thrive. This ecosystem would support early educators to become innovative and entrepreneurial leaders through coursework, innovator fellowships, and access to financial, human, and through intellectual capital to turn good ideas into high-impact improvements in ECE.

Policies, Funding, and Systems

Last, at the most distal level of the ecosystem, are the policies, funding streams, and systems that influence ECE programs and staff. How would these policies and systems need to be different if they were to support early educator and entrepreneurial leadership? Funding is certainly central. Early educators earn abysmally low salaries, and therefore access to scholarships or free leadership development coursework and programs is essential. Our post-master's certificate leadership program was free to educators for 4 years, thanks to funding from the Massachusetts Department of Early Education and Care through its Race to the Top Early Learning Challenge grant. During that time, so many educators applied that admission to the program was more competitive than admission to any of our other early education academic programs. However, when the grant ended, as so often happens, we saw a drop in applications. The financial support was essential in enabling the participation of early educators. We quickly turned to foundations to fill that gap in financial supports for educators.

Early educator entrepreneurs also need access to financing for facilities improvements and development and testing of innovations. Funding should come from both public and private sources. For example, there is very little philanthropic funding targeting leadership development in the birth-to-5 ECE sector, and we need to raise awareness that leadership is just as important in ECE as in all other educational sectors.

Professional development and quality improvement policy must be updated to include the use of models like the Breakthrough Series Collaborative, which recognize and elevate the voices of early educators in the change process, and which understand that we cannot transform program quality when we try to change only one part of the whole.

The ECE profession and policymakers frequently talk about the need to build a more unified system to overcome the disjointed fragmentation of ECE funding, government agencies, and policies (Kagan & Kauerz, 2012). We do need a better system. Our current system is complicated for providers, expensive for parents, and insufficiently funded and resourced to deliver high quality equitably. However, not all systems are good systems. As we work to streamline and standardize some functions of the system, we should not lose the strengths that are currently present.

What are those strengths and unique features of the ECE sector? ECE is a system built on parental choice in a market made up of a wide range of program models, types, and curricular approaches. Parents of babies very often choose home-based providers who speak the primary language of the family. Parents may choose a provider in their neighborhood, with staff who reflect the culture of the families served. While this market is far from perfect, its strength lies in its capacity to include linguistically and culturally diverse programs and educational models. It offers flexibility for ECE providers to offer different kinds of curricular or educational models. This flexibility enables diversity and preserves the capacity for innovation in ECE.

If we look at K–12 education, the system itself too often becomes the barrier. Educators and other innovators in K–12 education often attempt to undo the system or dismantle it or work around it, because the system gets in the way of innovation and improvement and thinking about problems in new ways. Schools can become entrenched in standardized systems and lose the freedom to be responsive, nimble, and agile in reflecting and responding to the needs of children and families. Early care and education is different.

ECE Sector Strengths

- Cultural and linguistic diversity of providers
- Diversity of program models and types of care
- Parental choice
- Flexibility and capacity to be responsive, innovative, and creative

There is quite a bit of room for creativity, innovation, and experimentation in this sector, so we should build our capacity to capitalize on that strength.

CONCLUSION

This chapter offers a model for a leadership development ecosystem capable of supporting early educators as change agents. Early educator leadership requires more than a stand-alone leadership development training program. Instead, early educators need ongoing access to a range of supports, resources, and networks. As a result of the successes of these kinds of ecosystems in other sectors, we know what many of these crucial components are, and we can build them into our own ECE leadership development ecosystem. In doing so, we strengthen not only the individual leadership capacities of educators, but also the capacity of ECE programs and systems to foster improvement and innovation. We build a culture of continuous learning, creativity, and innovation.

CHAPTER 10

A Leadership Ecosystem in Action

Imagine an experienced early educator or family child-care business owner with an idea about how to do things better. Now imagine that she could go to her local ECE leadership and innovation network, meet with others who share common ideas, and talk with local experts and mentors who provide advice to advance her idea. With these supports, she might test her idea on a small scale where she works, develop it further, and join an entrepreneurial leadership fellowship program. She might decide to stay in the field, motivated by her renewed professionalism and opportunities to learn and grow. She might move into a formal leadership position, or apply to an ECE innovation accelerator, and become part of a cohort of educators co-creating solutions, making change, and transforming the field. Now imagine hundreds and thousands of these educators and ECE business owners, convening and mobilizing collectively, a powerful leadership corps transforming our field. All of this is possible, and it is already happening at scale in other sectors. Right now in ECE, we lack a much-needed robust leadership development ecosystem. This book describes what this ecosystem might look like. Many of its components are well-developed in other sectors, which creates opportunities for ECE to learn and to test cross-sector collaborations.

A group of alumni from our leadership program approached me several years ago with a bold idea to build this ecosystem here. As a result of the passion and insight of many early educator leaders, we began to design and test key components of the ecosystem at a state and local level at our Institute for Early Education Leadership and Innovation at UMass Boston. The Institute, which is in its early developmental stages, was founded with a single mission: to leverage the power of diverse leadership from within the ECE field to transform early childhood learning opportunities and elevate the talented and diverse early childhood workforce. At UMass Boston, we engage over 300 early educators each year who represent the diversity of our workforce, communities, and the mixed-delivery system in ECE. Ultimately, by mobilizing this entrepreneurial leadership corps, the Institute seeks to close opportunity gaps and ensure that all young children get a great start in life. This chapter shares the early lessons we are learning about building this ecosystem as we test, grow, and collaborate with both existing and new partners.

Three Core Strategies to Strengthen ECE Leadership

1. Catalyzing leadership within the field
2. Connecting people within and across sectors
3. Co-creating new knowledge about how to systematically support the leadership of early educators and further professionalize the field

KEY STRATEGIES

We have focused on three core strategies to build an ecosystem to strengthen leadership in ECE. These strategies represent our theory of change about what it will take to deliver on our mission and its goal to close opportunity gaps for young children and their families. Below I define each strategy.

1. Catalyze the creative and entrepreneurial leadership development of early educators as the force for change. We learned how important it is to make the leadership of early educators visible, both within and beyond our field. As early educators come to define their own leadership identity, they encounter new possibilities and can become mobilized to take action. Geoff Mulgan (2006), a professor at the London School of Economics and former director of the Young Foundation, shares this insight, "Some of the most effective methods for cultivating social innovation start from the presumption that people are competent interpreters of their own lives and competent solvers of their own problems" (p. 150). Making early educator leadership possible requires that we discard old, deficit-oriented narratives about our workforce and its capacity to lead, create solutions, and contribute new ideas to the world. We must make the leadership of early educators more visible. The leadership of our program alumni has enhanced the lives of the children and families they serve, and it also has shifted perceptions, within and beyond the field, about the possibilities of early educator entrepreneurial leadership. These impacts highlight the multiplier effort of leadership development, which has yet to be tapped at scale in ECE.

2. Connect people, sectors, and systems to bring together the best science and expertise to infuse the ECE sector with skilled leadership, improve quality, and leverage technology to facilitate rapid generation and dissemination of new knowledge. We tend to operate in silos, independent of other disciplines or sectors that may have complementary or relevant knowledge, ideas, and solutions. When we connect across these boundaries, we create opportunities to leverage the insights and wisdom of others to advance our field. When it comes to leadership development, this is especially true because so many other industries and disciplines have invested in advancing science and practice about leadership. Much of this book seeks to do just that—to cross those boundaries and build bridges that enable the cross-fertilization of ideas, theories, and research. Each of the programs and activities at our Institute seeks to capitalize on these points of connection.

3. Co-Create innovative and sustainable systems change by convening educators, thought leaders, researchers, policymakers, funders, and other practitioners across traditional disciplinary boundaries to generate new knowledge. Through these efforts, we co-create the supportive policies and systems that sustain the ecosystem. This book calls out the dearth of research on leadership, and especially the entrepreneurial leadership of early educators. Through research and evaluation, and their strategic dissemination, we can build an evidence base about what works and how to improve and strengthen a leadership development ecosystem in ECE.

The Institute for Early Education Leadership and Innovation acts on this theory of change through its programming and activities, all of which serve to catalyze, connect, and co-create the leadership we need.

One key element of the Entrepreneurial Leadership Training is the leadership certificate program which I have described previously in this book. Next I highlight three specific programmatic elements: our Leadership Forum, part of the Research and Policy Center; the Innovation Lab and Accelerator, our newest program; and the ECE Small Business Innovation Center in our Training program.

THE LEADERSHIP FORUM

We launched the Leadership Forum on Early Education Research, Policy, and Practice in 2012, as part of our effort to develop a network among the educators in our leadership programs and early education leaders and stakeholders at the local, state, and national levels. This annual event creates a forum to share expertise and engage in dialogue and networking about current research, policy, practice, and leadership in the field. It was designed

Three Core Areas of Programming

1. Our Research and Policy Center
2. A new Innovation Lab and Accelerator
3. Entrepreneurial Leadership Training

to assist educators in building relationships with prominent leaders in the field by connecting them to research and educational opportunities and networks. Each year, the educators who are graduating from our entrepreneurial leadership training programs are featured at the forum. Each presents his/her "change project"—a concrete plan to drive change to achieve a specific outcome, guided by a theory of change, and a set of action steps and measures of progress. During the forum, attendees enter into dialogue with the presenting educators, asking questions, offering suggestions, and making connections to people and organizations that can enhance the educators' leadership on their change projects.

Educators report that they made some of the most important professional connections of their careers at the Leadership Forum. Attendees frequently report feeling transformed by witnessing and engaging with the leadership of these early educators. I have seen how powerful it is when we make early educator leadership visible, so the world can see how very possible and real it is. Kim Syman is a managing partner at New Profit, a national nonprofit venture philanthropy fund whose stated mission is to break down the barriers that stand between people and opportunity in America. She has been a supportive partner of our Institute. She attended our most recent Leadership Forum and facilitated one of the small-group discussions that took place during a design session we held prior to launching the Institute. We produced a video for the Institute that highlights the Leadership Forum, in which Kim shared her reflections: "What I saw in the students at the Leadership Forum absolutely blew me away. Every single student I met had so much energy for the thing they were working on. What I saw was a real resolve on the part of the students to make something happen . . . they wanted to go out in the community and change things" (UMass Boston, 2016). The Leadership Forum has been a clear catalyst for action, has connected educators with powerful leadership networks, and has served as a platform for sharing and co-creating knowledge and practice innovation.

THE INNOVATION LAB AND ACCELERATOR

To build a leadership development ecosystem requires cross-sector expertise and know-how, so we can capitalize on advances in other fields while applying and adapting them appropriately for our own field. It requires opportunities for educators to join networks and cohorts, and gain access to mentors and other resources. The Innovation Lab and Accelerator model is a good example of how other fields have developed these capacities (Dempwolf et al., 2014). My colleague Dr. Banu Özkazanç-Pan is an associate professor of management at UMass Boston and an expert on entrepreneurial ecosystems that are inclusive of women and minorities (Clark Muntean & Özkazanç-Pan, 2014, 2016; Knowlton, Özkazanç-Pan, Clark

Muntean, & Motoyama, 2015). She is the director and co-designer of our first-of-its-kind innovation accelerator for early educators at the Institute for Early Education Leadership and Innovation. A laboratory for growing educators' innovative solutions to improve early learning opportunities, this accelerator is an example of connecting across sectors, taking a tested approach from one sector and adapting and applying it to ECE.

An innovation accelerator is a structure for providing the kinds of resources and supports I have just described, such as intellectual, human, and financial capital. In the business sector, accelerators have fostered entrepreneurial growth and economic development. ECE business owners and innovators have unique needs based on their customer base, business models, revenue streams, demographic characteristics, and the economic status of their clients and their workforce. Our accelerator is a local ecosystem, one we will grow through a process of testing and refinement and scaling. What our accelerator does is to engage cohorts of educators and provide them with individualized supports and resources over a period of time, typically 1 year. These resources include mentoring, consulting, executive coaching, and networking with key stakeholders and funders. The accelerator is a vehicle for generating and refining ideas, supporting innovations, and showcasing and spreading what works.

This accelerator is a community-driven model that fosters innovation in the local ECE sector and addresses the unique and specific challenges at the intersection of business and quality. Leadership development and innovation methods such as accelerators have revolutionized so many other industries. In ECE, these methods will have a powerful and multiplying effect, opening doors to advancing quality and other improvements.

ECE SMALL BUSINESS INNOVATION CENTER

The Institute also is exploring ways to collaborate and partner with existing leadership and entrepreneurial programs and ecosystems to maximize resources and efficiencies. Why create something new from scratch if we can design ways to make some of the existing resources more inclusive and aligned with the needs of early educators? For example, we built a partnership with a national urban entrepreneurial business growth program called Inner City Capital Connections, a program of the Initiative for a Competitive Inner City (ICIC). Founded in 1994 by Harvard Business School Professor Michael Porter, ICIC is a national nonprofit research and advisory organization and a leading authority on U.S. inner-city economies and the businesses that thrive there. Through this partnership, we will test a model for collaboratively supporting a cohort of early education small business owners in the Inner City Capital Connection program. We expect that ultimately the best ecosystem for ECE leadership development will offer a combination of ECE-specific, specialized resources, programming, and networks, and also collaborative partnerships like this one to connect with the more mainstream business and leadership ecosystems.

We also run entrepreneurial leadership training for family child-care and small ECE business owners. These programs have the capability to increase ECE business acumen, technology skills, entrepreneurial leadership, quality improvement knowledge and capacity, and early educator innovation. The Institute creates a place for educators to network and co-create innovative solutions to business and quality improvement challenges. It establishes an inclusive entrepreneurial ecosystem to improve quality and business stability by creating inclusive entrepreneurial support systems that meet the needs of the early education sector.

Based on pilots of the entrepreneurial leadership training programs we have been testing over the past few years, the programs have had transformative impact. The percentage of ECE business owners reporting that they have a budget for their business increased from 28% to 72% after the training; 78% of participants reported having a business plan post-training versus 22% pre-training. After completing entrepreneurship training and coaching, one director said that, after 30 years in the field, she could now manage her finances well enough to raise teachers' salaries. Other participants agreed they were better prepared to manage their fiscal responsibilities, and many reported increases in enrollment and revenue. One leadership program graduate explained, "I don't want to just be someone who is on a committee full of people griping about how hard it is to be in the field. I want to actually be a vehicle for change. I want to be a leader in the full[est sense of the word] and make something happen." Another reflected, "This program provided me with the knowledge, network, and confidence to see myself as an agent of change, and now it is our opportunity to implement all that learning and transform it into something really impactful in the field of early childhood education."

A field-wide leadership development ecosystem will amplify these results. Our program alumni are forming a powerful leadership corps, becoming successful role models and mentors supporting the next generation of leaders and entrepreneurs. They represent a diverse corps of leaders who are participating in early care and education policy, practice, and financing reform and innovation. As key leaders in the field, these educators bring deep experience, a wide range of educational backgrounds, and a wealth of diversity in race, class, ethnicity, religion, and language to the table. All of these field-based, expert practitioners are critically important voices for transforming quality in early care and education businesses.

Early educator leaders and entrepreneurs depend on a leadership development ecosystem for the supports they need to leverage their practical experience into insights to improve the field, implement new ideas, and influence public policy and other levers of widespread impact.

CONCLUSION

It is time to build an infrastructure for the field to support the passionate, creative, and smart leadership of experienced early educators. There are many components to building a strong leadership development ecosystem that we are actively testing now at our Institute. By creating this ecosystem at a local level, it becomes deeply embedded in the community, building local capacity and ownership for change and the creation of solutions. Local leaders see the potential and promise in their communities, where so many others see only deficits and problems. These educators are uniquely positioned to drive change more rapidly, more effectively, and more sustainably. Local solutions—built from capacity within the community—have lasting impact. As we test and adapt and refine this model, we are learning about how to grow it in other communities in ways that retain local ownership while at the same time building connectivity with the larger ecosystem. It is our vision that these early educators from within the field will lead transformative changes that strengthen our workforce and dramatically increase opportunity for all young children and their families to thrive.

CHAPTER 11

Conclusion

The Leadership of Early Educators

The early educators represented in this book are trailblazers who take action every day to ensure that all young children get a great start in life. Their stories offer a new narrative about the power and possibilities of early educator leadership. They challenge many of the long-held stereotypes about this workforce and its capacity for change. My work with these educators, and my 20 years' prior experience working with children, families, and other educators in ECE programs, have convinced me that immense untapped potential for improvement and innovation lies within the ECE workforce.

Despite repeated calls for more leadership development, the ECE field still lags behind almost all other fields in this regard. Educators are rarely treated as leaders or co-creators of change. Instead, they often are treated as passive adopters of change. But it doesn't have to be this way. Other fields are learning how to improve by respecting and elevating the expertise of those who work on the front lines of service delivery. Leadership and innovation drive success in business, the military, healthcare, technology, and the public sector. Leadership development has the potential to reap similarly dramatic benefits in ECE. Yet almost no opportunities currently exist to develop and support leadership from within the diverse ECE workforce. Without these opportunities, experienced and creative thinkers are moving out of the field, depriving us of our richest resource: the talent and innovative ideas of early educators.

Leadership development and innovation have revolutionized so many other sectors. It is time to extend these supports to ECE, where they will have a powerful and multiplying effect, unleashing our capacity to improve and strengthen child care and early learning opportunities for children and their families. This book has shared many specific strategies, methods, and models for unleashing the potential of early educators to inform and design change.

This book makes an urgent call to focus leadership development approaches and systems toward the educators working most closely with children and families. It calls for an end to the leadership development gap in our field. If we shift our paradigm about who can be leaders, and develop more inclusive pathways for this leadership, we will revolutionize our field.

I have presented the framework for an ecosystem to support and nurture innovative, entrepreneurial, and skilled early educators as leaders and change-makers. Experienced early educators understand better than anyone else the barriers to and solutions for transforming quality. Making their leadership visible elevates the professionalism of the ECE workforce and adds fuel to the ongoing efforts to establish equitable compensation.

We will grow this early educator leadership corps by building an ecosystem that cultivates the leadership needed to address the challenges and the transformative opportunities we face. This ecosystem supports leaders at all levels, throughout their careers, individually and collectively. It supports networks of ECE programs and creates hubs of innovation that foster a culture of learning. Educators and programs will have access to the full range of improvement and innovation supports, from the latest cutting-edge research knowledge to the networks, mentors, and financial capital that fuel innovation. Systems and policies will support cross-sector partnerships and nontraditional alliances that will connect ECE with the many existing resources for leadership and innovation learning and experimentation.

As early educators, we share a vision of a world made better when all children get a great start in life. A moral imperative of our democracy is to ensure that all children start life with equal opportunities to achieve success. High-quality ECE nurtures children's love of learning, prevents the opportunity gap, and saves society $10 for every $1 invested. High-quality child care and early education provide the foundation that can equalize children's opportunities to succeed in school and in life. The science is clear—when children start off strong, they are far more likely to continue strong.

We know that we have work to do to improve early care and education. Right now, too many ECE programs struggle when it comes to quality. And in many communities, the children most in need have the least access to high-quality programs. This inequity, so early in life, fuels the opportunity gap. We must do better.

What if we were all 10 times bolder? What would we be doing right now, individually, where we work, and in our profession? Stephanie is a family child-care provider and one of so many smart and talented early educators I've had the privilege to teach. As she boldly articulated, "We as a profession need an army of leaders willing to fight for change in order to make the difference that will last."

Early educators, in partnership with families and communities, are building the foundation for our future. Strengthening leadership will strengthen that foundation. When I reflect on the expertise and leadership of early educators, I often think of Mei, a teacher who participated in one of my research studies. Mei told me about the most difficult family she had encountered in her many years as a preschool teacher at a child-care center. John was a 3-year-old in her class whose frequent challenging behaviors had been too much for his mother, Marianne. Marianne seemed to have given up on

John—he was too much to handle and nothing seemed to work. Mei tried everything to engage with Marianne and to partner with her to support John and the whole family. For a while, nothing seemed to work. It appeared that Marianne had no interest in partnering with Mei. But through Mei's caring persistence and deep respect for both John and his mother, she managed to foster a trusting relationship with Marianne. Mei helped Marianne understand John's behaviors in a new way and to see his strengths again. Mei and Marianne shared the funny things John did and said, reminding them both of his wonderful sense of humor.

One day, through tears, Marianne revealed to Mei, "You helped me love my child again." Mei's story exemplifies the powerful role early educators play in the most important relationships and developmental period of children's lives. Early educators like Mei act boldly every day, when they refuse to give up, persist despite obstacles, and apply their insights to create new solutions to better serve children and families.

The complex and persistent challenges we face call for creative solutions, informed and driven by early educators seeding change in local communities across the country. It is time to embrace the entrepreneurial leadership of early educators as a transformative force for our field. As one leadership program alumna concluded, "If we train strong and confident teachers, we can change the world."

References

Ackerman, D. J. (2008). Continuity of care, professional community, and the policy context: Potential benefits for infant and toddler teachers' professional development. *Early Education and Development, 19*(5), 753–722.

Ackoff, R. L. (2010). Beyond continual improvement: Systems-based improvement [Video file]. Retrieved from youtube.com/watch?v=_pcuzRq-rDU&feature=youtube

Ackoff, R. L., & Rovin, S. (2003). *Redesigning society*. Stanford, CA: Stanford Business Books.

Adams, G., Tout, K., & Zaslow, M. (2007). *Early care and education for children in low-income families: Patterns of use, quality, and potential policy implications.* Washington, DC: Urban Institute.

Agosti, J., Conradi, L., Halladay Goldman, J., & Langan, H. (2013). *Using trauma-informed child welfare practice to improve placement stability* [Breakthrough Series Collaborative: Promising practices and lessons learned]. Los Angeles, CA & Durham, NC: National Center for Child Traumatic Stress.

Aikens, N., Bush, C., Gleason, P., Malone, L., & Tarullo, L. (2016). *Tracking quality in Head Start classrooms: FACES 2006 to FACES 2014* (Research Brief). Retrieved from acf.hhs.gov/sites/default/files/opre/faces_tracking_quality_in_head_start_100716_b508.pdf

Ancona, D., & Bresman, H. (2007). *X-teams: How to build teams that lead, innovate and succeed.* Boston, MA: Harvard Business School Publishing.

Anzaldúa, G., Keating, A. L., Mignolo, W. D., Silverblatt, I., & Saldívar-Hull, S. (2009). *The Gloria Anzaldúa reader*. Durham, NC: Duke University Press.

Apple, P., & McMullen, M. B. (2007). Envisioning the impact of decisions made about early childhood professional development systems by different constituent groups. *Contemporary Issues in Early Childhood, 8*(3), 255–264.

Arbour, M., Yoshikawa, H., Atwood, S., Duran Mellado, F. R., Godoy Ossa, F., Trevino Villareal, E., & Snow, C. E. (2016). *Improving quality and child outcomes in early childhood education by redefining the role afforded to teachers in professional development: A continuous quality improvement learning collaborative among public preschools in Chile*. Evanston, IL: Society for Research on Educational Effectiveness. Retrieved from files.eric.ed.gov/fulltext/ED566990.pdf

Armstrong, L. J., Kinney, K. C., & Clayton, L. H. (2009). Getting started: Leadership opportunities for beginning early childhood teachers. *Dimensions of Early Childhood, 37*(3), 11–17.

Backer, P. M., Kiser, L. J., Gillham, J. E., & Smith, J. (2015). The Maryland resilience Breakthrough Series Collaborative: A quality improvement initiative for children's mental health services providers. *Psychiatric Services, 66*(8), 778–780. doi:10.1176/appi.ps.201500036

Bailie, R. S., Si, D., O Donoghue, L., & Dowden, M. (2007). Indigenous health: Effective and sustainable health services through continuous quality improvement. *Medical Journal of Australia, 186*(10), 525–527. Retrieved from mja.com.au/journal/2007/186/10/indigenous-health-effective-and-sustainable-health-services-through-continuous?inline=true

Bandura, A. (1977). Self-efficacy: Toward a unifying theory of behavioral change. *Psychological Review, 84*, 191–215.

Berwick, D. M. (1994). Eleven worthy aims for clinical leadership of health system reform. *Jama, 272*(10), 797–802. doi:10.1001/jama.1994.03520100059034

Bitton, A., Ellner, A., Pabo, E., Stout, S., Sugarman, J. R., Sevin, C., . . . & Phillips, R. S. (2014). The Harvard Medical School Academic Innovations Collaborative: Transforming primary care practice and education. *Academic Medicine, 89*(9), 1239–1244. doi:10.1097/ACM.0000000000000410

Bloom, P. J. (1991). Child care centers as organizations: A social systems perspective. *Child and Youth Care Forum, 20*(5), 313–333.

Bloom, P. J. (2005). *Blueprint for action: Achieving center-based change through staff development*. Lake Forest, IL: New Horizons.

Bloom, P., & Bella, J. (2005). Investment in leadership training—the payoff for early childhood education. *Young Children, 60*(1), 32–40.

Bloom, P. J., & Sheerer, M. (1992). The effect of leadership training on child care program quality. *Early Childhood Research Quarterly, 7*(4), 579–594.

Boller, K., Tarrant, K., & Schaack, D. D. (2014). *Early care and education quality improvement: A typology of intervention approaches* (OPRE Research Report No. 2014-36). Washington, DC: Office of Planning, Research and Evaluation, Administration for Children and Families, U.S. Department of Health and Human Services.

Boston EQUIP. (2010). *Early care and education in Boston: 2009 community profiles report*. Boston, MA: Associated Early Care and Education.

Boushon, B., Provost, L., Gagnon, J., & Carver, P. (2006). Using a virtual Breakthrough Series Collaborative to improve access in primary care. *The Joint Commission Journal on Quality and Patient Safety, 32*(10), 573–584. doi:10.1016/S1553-7250(06)32075-2

Bradley, B. H., Postlethwaite, B. E., Klotz, A. C., Hamdani, M. R., & Brown, K. G. (2012). Reaping the benefits of task conflict in teams: The critical role of team psychological safety climate. *Journal of Applied Psychology, 97*(1), 151. doi:10.1037/a0024200

Bronfenbrenner, U. (1979). *The ecology of human development*. Cambridge, MA: Harvard University Press.

Bronfenbrenner, U., & Morris, P. (1998). The ecology of developmental processes. In R. M. Lerner (Ed.), *Handbook of child psychology, Vol. 1: Theoretical models of human development* (5th ed., pp. 993–1028). New York, NY: Wiley.

Bryk, A. S., Gomez, L. M., Grunow, A., & LeMahieu, P. B. (2015). *Learning to improve: How America's schools can get better at getting better*. Cambridge, MA: Harvard Education Press.

Bureau of Labor Statistics. (2014). Elementary, middle, and high school principals (2014–2015). *Occupational outlook handbook*. Retrieved from bls.gov/ooh/management/elementary-middle-and-high-school-principals.htm

Calás, M. B., Smircich, L., & Bourne, K. A. (2009). Extending the boundaries: Reframing "Entrepreneurship as Social Change" through feminist perspectives. *Academy of Management Review, 34*(3), 552–569. doi:10.5465/amr.2009.40633597

Cameron, C., Mooney, A., & Moss, P. (2002). The child care workforce: Current conditions and future directions. *Critical Social Policy, 22*(4), 572–595.

Cameron, H. (2012). Social entrepreneurs in the social innovation ecosystem. In A. Nicholls & A. Murdock (Eds.), *Social innovation: Blurring boundaries to reconfigure markets* (pp. 199–220). London, UK: Palgrave Macmillan UK.

Cameron, K. S. (2008). Paradox in positive organizational change. *The Journal of Applied Behavioral Science, 44*(1), 7–24. doi:10.1177/0021886308314703

Cameron, K. S., & Spreitzer, G. M. (2012). *The Oxford handbook of positive organizational scholarship*. New York, NY: Oxford University Press.

Cancian, F. (2000). Paid emotional care: Organizational forms that encourage nurturance. In M. H. Meyer (Ed.), *Care work: Gender, class, and the welfare state* (pp. 136–148). New York, NY: Routledge.

Carr, V., Johnson, L. J., & Corkwell, C. (2009). Principle-centered leadership in early childhood education. *Dimensions of Early Childhood, 37*(3), 25–32.

Child Care in America: 2016 State Fact Sheets. (2016). Retrieved from usa.childcareaware.org/wp-content/uploads/2016/07/2016-Fact-Sheets-Full-Report-02-27-17.pdf

Christensen, C. M., Johnson, C. W., & Horn, M. B. (2008). *Disrupting class: How disruptive innovation will change the way the world learns*. New York, NY: McGraw-Hill.

Christiansen, L. C., & Higgs, M. (2010). What makes change implementation successful? A study of the behaviors of change leaders in Denmark. Retrieved from eprints.soton.ac.uk/id/eprint/183743

Clark Muntean, S., & Özkazanç-Pan, B. (2014). Social networking and technology-focused business incubators: A critical gender perspective. *Academy of Management Proceedings, 2014*(1). doi:10.5465/AMBPP.2014.14177abstract

Clark Muntean, S., & Özkazanç-Pan, B. (2016). Feminist perspectives on social entrepreneurship: Critique and new directions. *International Journal of Gender and Entrepreneurship, 8*(3), 221–241. doi:10.1108/IJGE-10-2014-0034

Coles, J., Dartnall, E., & Astbury, J. (2013). "Preventing the pain" when working with family and sexual violence in primary care. *International Journal of Family Medicine, 2013*. doi: 10.1155/2013/198578

Connors, M. C. (2016). Creating cultures of learning: A theoretical model of effective early care and education policy. *Early Childhood Research Quarterly, 36*, 32–45. doi:10.1016/j.ecresq.2015.12.005

Couros, G. (2015). *The innovator's mindset: Empower learning, unleash talent, and lead a culture of creativity*. San Diego, CA: Dave Burgess Consulting.

Dana, N. F., & Yendol-Hoppey, D. (2005). Becoming an early childhood teacher leader and an advocate for social justice: A phenomenological interview study. *Journal of Early Childhood Teacher Education, 26*(3), 191–206.

Darling-Hammond, L., Wei, R. C., Andree, A., Richardson, N., & Orphanos, S. (2009). *Professional learning in the learning profession: A status report on teacher development in the United States and abroad*. Stanford, CA: National Staff Development Council.

Deming, W. E. (1986). *Out of the crisis*. Cambridge, MA: Massachusetts Institute of Technology, Center for Advanced Engineering Study.

Dempwolf, S., Auer, J., & D'Ippolito, M. (2014). Innovation accelerators: Defining characteristics among startup assistance organizations. Retrieved from sba.gov/sites/default/files/rs425-Innovation-Accelerators-Report-FINAL.pdf

Derrick-Mills, T., Sandstrom, H., Pettijohn, S. L., Fyffe, S., & Koulish, J. (2014). *Data use for continuous quality improvement: What the Head Start field can learn from other disciplines: A literature review and conceptual framework* (OPRE Report No. 2014-77). Washington, DC: Office of Planning, Research and Evaluation, Administration for Children and Families, U.S. Department of Health and Human Services.

Dollard, M. F., & Bakker, A. B. (2010). Psychosocial safety climate as a precursor to conducive work environments, psychological health problems, and employee engagement. *Journal of Occupational and Organizational Psychology, 83*(3), 579–599. doi:10.1348/096317909X470690

Douglass, A. (2011). Improving family engagement: The organizational context and its influence on partnering with parents in formal child care settings. *Early Childhood Research & Practice, 13*(2). Retrieved from ecrp.uiuc.edu/v13n2/douglass.html

Douglass, A. (2014). Resilience in change: Positive perspectives on the dynamics of change in early childhood systems. *Journal of Early Childhood Research, 14*(2), 211–225. doi:10.1177/1476718x14555704

Douglass, A. (2016a). *Impact of the post master's certificate program in early education research, policy, and practice: Program evaluation report to the Massachusetts Department of Early Education and Care*. Boston, MA: University of Massachusetts Boston.

Douglass, A. (2016b). *Improving trauma informed practice in ECE: The Breakthrough Series Collaborative methodology for quality improvement* (evaluation report submitted to the Boston Public Health Commission Defending Childhood Initiative). Boston, MA: University of Massachusetts Boston.

Douglass, A. (2016c). *Strengthening leadership from the field, for the field: Key research findings* (Leadership Research Brief No. 3). Boston, MA: University of Massachusetts Boston.

Douglass, A. (2016d). Trauma and young children. In D. Couchenour & J. Chrisman (Eds.), *The Sage encyclopedia of contemporary early childhood education* (Vol. 3, pp. 1395–1396). Thousand Oaks, CA: Sage. doi:10.4135/9781483340333.n421

Douglass, A., Benson, S., Hodges-Hunter, D., Wiles, D., & Stardrum, R. (2015). *Successful inclusion of family child care providers in higher education degree programs and courses: A research-to-practice guide*. Washington, DC: Early Educator Central, Administration for Children and Families, U.S. Department of Health and Human Services.

Douglass, A., Carter, A., Smith, F., & Killins, S. (2015). Training together: State policy and collective participation in early educator professional development.

New England Journal of Public Policy, 27(1). Retrieved from scholarworks.umb.edu/nejpp/vol27/iss1/5

Douglass, A., & Gittell, J. (2012). Transforming professionalism: Relational bureaucracy and parent–teacher partnerships in child care settings. *Journal of Early Childhood Research, 10*(3), 267–281. doi:10.1177/1476718x12442067

Douglass, A., & Klerman, L. (2012). The Strengthening Families Initiative and child care quality improvement: How Strengthening Families influenced change in child care programs in one state. *Early Education & Development, 23*(3), 373–392. doi:10.1080/10409289.2012.666193

Doyle, S., Agosti, J., Rivers, S., & Douglass, A. (2016). *Early care and education Breakthrough Series Collaborative: A toolkit.* Boston, MA: Boston Public Health Commission Defending Childhood Initiative.

Dutton, J. E., & Ragins, B. R. (2007). *Exploring positive relationships at work: Building a theoretical and research foundation.* Mahwah, NJ: Erlbaum.

Eaton, S. C. (2000). Beyond "unloving care": Linking human resource management and patient care quality in nursing homes. *International Journal of Human Resource Management, 11*(3), 591–616. doi:10.1080/095851900339774

Ebert, L., Amaya-Jackson, L., Markiewicz, J. M., Kisiel, C., & Fairbank, J. A. (2012). Use of the Breakthrough Series Collaborative to support broad and sustained use of evidence-based trauma treatment for children in community practice settings. *Administration and Policy in Mental Health and Mental Health Services Research, 39*(3), 187–199.

Edmondson, A. (1999). Psychological safety and learning behavior in work teams. *Administrative Science Quarterly, 44*(2), 350–383.

Edmondson, A. C., & Lei, Z. (2014). Psychological safety: The history, renaissance, and future of an interpersonal construct. *Annual Review of Organizational Psychology and Organizational Behavior, 1*(1), 23–43. doi:10.1146/annurev-orgpsych-031413-091305

Education Pioneers & Koya Leadership Partners. (2014). *From intention to action: Building diverse, inclusive teams in education to deepen impact.* Retrieved from educationpioneers.org/blog/intention-action-building-diverse-inclusive-teams-education-deepen-impact

Ely, R. J., Ibarra, H., & Kolb, D. M. (2011). Taking gender into account: Theory and design for women's leadership development programs. *Academy of Management Learning & Education, 10*(3), 474–493. doi:10.5465/amle.2010.0046

Fisher, B., & Tronto, J. (1990). Toward a feminist theory of caring. In E. K. Abel & M. K. Nelson (Eds.), *Circles of care: Work and identity in women's lives* (pp. 35–62). Albany, NY: State University of New York Press.

Fletcher, J. K. (1999). *Disappearing acts: Gender, power, and relational practice at work.* Cambridge, MA: MIT Press.

Fletcher, J. K. (2004). A paradox of postheroic leadership: An essay on gender, power, and transformational change. *The Leadership Quarterly, 15*, 647–661. doi:10.1016/j.leaqua.2004.07.004

Foster-Fishman, P. G., & Behrens, T. R. (2007). Systems change reborn: Rethinking our theories, methods, and efforts in human services reform and community-based change. *American Journal of Community Psychology, 39*(3/4), 191–196. doi:10.1007/s10464-007-9104-5

Foster-Fishman, P. G., Nowell, B., & Yang, H. (2007). Putting the system back into systems change: A framework for understanding and changing organizational and community systems. *American Journal of Community Psychology, 39*(3-4), 197–215. doi:10.1007/s10464-007-9109-0

French, L., & Wagner, B. D. (2010). Motivation, work satisfaction, and teacher change among early childhood teachers. *Journal of Research in Childhood Education, 24*, 152–171.

Fullan, M. (2008). School leadership's unfinished agenda: Integrating individual and organizational development. *Education Week*. Retrieved from edweek.org/ew/articles/2008/04/09/32fullan.h27.html

George, J. M. (2007). Creativity in organizations. *The Academy of Management Annals, 1*(1), 439–477. doi: 10.1080/078559814

Gittell, J. H. (2002). Relationships between service providers and their impact on customers. *Journal of Service Research, 4*(4), 299–311. doi:10.1177/1094670502004004007

Gittell, J. H. (2003). *The Southwest Airlines way: Using the power of relationships to achieve high performance.* New York, NY: McGraw-Hill.

Gittell, J. H. (2008). Relationships and resilience. *The Journal of Applied Behavioral Science, 44*(1), 25–47. doi:10.1177/0021886307311469

Gittell, J. H. (2016). *Transforming relationships for high performance: The power of relational coordination*: Stanford, CA: Stanford University Press.

Gittell, J. H., & Douglass, A. (2012). Relational bureaucracy: Structuring reciprocal relationships into roles. *Academy of Management Review, 37*(4), 709–733. doi:10.5465/amr.2010.0438

Gittell, J. H., Seidner, R., & Wimbush, J. (2010). A relational model of how high-performance work systems work. *Organization Science, 21*(2), 490–506. doi:10.1287/orsc.1090.0446

Glisson, C. (2007). Assessing and changing organizational culture and climate for effective services. *Research on Social Work Practice, 17*(6), 736–747. doi:10.1177/1049731507301659

Glisson, C., & Hemmelgarn, A. (1998). The effects of organizational climate and interorganizational coordination on the quality and outcomes of children's service systems. *Child Abuse & Neglect, 22*(5), 401–421. doi:10.1016/S0145-2134(98)00005-2

Goffin, S. G. (2013). *Early childhood education for a new era: Leading for our profession.* New York, NY: Teachers College Press.

Goffin, S., & Janke, M. (2013). *Early childhood education leadership development compendium: A view of the current landscape.* Washington, DC: Goffin Strategy Group.

Goffin, S. G., & Washington, V. (2007). *Ready or not: Leadership choices in early care and education.* New York, NY: Teachers College Press.

Golden-Biddle, K., & Mao, J. (2012). What makes an organizational change process positive? In K. S. Cameron & G. M. Spreitzer (Eds.), *The Oxford handbook of positive organizational scholarship* (pp. 763–772). New York, NY: Oxford University Press.

Goldstein, L. S. (2007). Beyond the DAP versus standards dilemma: Examining the unforgiving complexity of kindergarten teaching in the United States. *Early Childhood Research Quarterly, 22*(1), 39–54.

Grieshaber, S. (2001). Advocacy and early childhood educators: Identity and cultural conflicts. In S. Grieshaber & G. Cannella (Eds.), *Embracing identities in early childhood education: Diversity and possibilities* (pp. 60–72). New York, NY: Teachers College Press.

Hadley, C. N. (2014). Emotional roulette? Symmetrical and asymmetrical emotion regulation outcomes from coworker interactions about positive and negative work events. *Human Relations, 67*(9), 1073–1094. doi:10.1177/0018726714529316

Halle, T., Metz, A., & Martinez-Beck, I. (Eds.). (2013). *Applying implementation science in early childhood programs and systems*. Baltimore, MD: Brookes.

Hamer, S. (2010). Developing an innovation ecosystem: A framework for accelerating knowledge transfer. *Journal of Management & Marketing in Healthcare, 3*(4), 248–255. doi:10.1179/175330310X12736578177607

Hargreaves, M. B. (2010). Evaluating system change: A planning guide. Available at mathematica-mpr.com/our-publications-and-findings/publications/evaluating-system-change-a-planning-guide

Harms, T., Cryer, D., & Clifford, R. (2005). *Early childhood environment rating scale–revised*. New York, NY: Teachers College Press.

Harms, T., Cryer, D., & Clifford, R. (2007). *Family child care environment rating scale–revised*. New York, NY: Teachers College Press.

Heckman, J. J. (2012). Invest in early childhood development: Reduce deficits, strengthen the economy. *The Heckman Equation, 7*.

Heikka, J., & Waniganayake, M. (2011). Pedagogical leadership from a distributed perspective within the context of early childhood education. *International Journal of Leadership in Education: Theory and Practice, 14*(4), 499–512. doi:10.1080/13603124.2011.577909

Hemmelgarn, A. L., Glisson, C., & Dukes, D. (2001). Emergency room culture and the emotional support component of family-centered care. *Children's Health Care, 30*(2), 93–110. doi:10.1207/S15326888CHC3002_2

Henderson-Kelly, L., & Pamphilon, B. (2000). Women's models of leadership in the childcare sector. *Australian Journal of Early Childhood, 25*(1), 8–12.

Hess, F. M. (2006). *Educational entrepreneurship: Realities, challenges, possibilities*. Cambridge, MA: Harvard Education Press.

Hesselbein, F., Shinseki, E. K., & Cavanagh, R. E. (2004). *Be, know, do: Leadership the army way*. San Francisco, CA: Jossey-Bass.

Hewlett, S., Marshall, M., & Sherbin, L. (2013, December). How diversity can drive innovation. *Harvard Business Review*. Retrieved from hbr.org/2013/12/how-diversity-can-drive-innovation

Hillemeier, M. M., Morgan, P. L., Farkas, G., & Maczuga, S. A. (2013). Quality disparities in child care for at-risk children: Comparing Head Start and non-Head Start settings. *Maternal and Child Health Journal, 17*(1), 180–188. doi:10.1007/s10995-012-0961-7

Hinitz, B.S.F. (Ed.). (2013). *The hidden history of early childhood education*. New York, NY: Routledge.

Hyson, M., & Whittaker, J. V. (2012). Professional development in early childhood systems. In S. L. Kagan & K. Kauerz (Eds.), *Early childhood systems: Transforming early learning* (pp. 104–118). New York, NY: Teachers College Press.

IDEO. (2015). *The fieldguide to human centered design*. Palo Alto, CA: Author.

Institute for Healthcare Improvement. (2003). *The breakthrough series: IHI's collaborative model for achieving breakthrough improvement*. Cambridge, MA: Institute for Healthcare Improvement.

Institute of Medicine and National Research Council. (2015). *Transforming the workforce for children birth through age 8: A unifying foundation*. Washington, DC: National Academies Press.

Janus, K. (2016, August 31). A call for inclusive entrepreneurship. *Stanford Social Innovation Review*. Retrieved from ssir.org/articles/entry/a_call_for_inclusive_entrepreneurship

Kagan, S. L., & Bowman, B. T. (1997). *Leadership in early care and education*. Washington, DC: National Association for the Education of Young Children.

Kagan, S. L., & Kauerz, K. (Eds.). (2012). *Early childhood systems: Transforming early learning*. New York, NY: Teachers College Press.

Kelley, T., & Kelley, D. (2012). Reclaim your creative confidence. *Harvard Business Review*. Retrieved from hbr.org/2012/12/reclaim-your-creative-confidence

Kilo, C. M. (1998). A framework for collaborative improvement: Lessons from the Institute for Healthcare Improvement's Breakthrough Series. *Quality Management in Healthcare, 6*(4), 1–14.

Knowlton, K., Özkazanç-Pan, B., Clark Muntean, S., & Motoyama, Y. (2015). Support organizations and remediating the gender gap in entrepreneurial ecosystems: A case study of St. Louis. doi:10.2139/ssrn.2685116

Komives, S. R., Lucas, N., & McMahon, T. R. (2013). *Exploring leadership: For college students who want to make a difference*. San Francisco, CA: Wiley.

Kunnari, I., & Ilomäki, L. (2016). Reframing teachers' work for educational innovation. *Innovations in Education and Teaching International, 53*(2), 167–178. doi:10.1080/14703297.2014.978351

Langley, G. J., Moen, R. D., Nolan, K. M., Nolan, T. W., Norman, C. L., & Provost, L. P. (2009). *The improvement guide: A practical approach to enhancing organizational performance* (2nd ed.). San Francisco, CA: Jossey-Bass.

Laschinger, H.K.S., Wong, C. A., & Grau, A. L. (2013). Authentic leadership, empowerment and burnout: A comparison in new graduates and experienced nurses. *Journal of Nursing Management, 21*(3), 541–552. doi:10.1111/j.1365-2834.2012.01375.x

LeMoine, S. (2008). *Workforce designs: A policy blueprint for state early childhood professional development systems*. Washington, DC: National Association for the Education of Young Children.

Leonard, J. (2013). *Innovation in the schoolhouse: Entrepreneurial leadership in education*. New York, NY: Rowman & Littlefield Education.

Lieberman, A., Campbell, C., & Yashkina, A. (2017). *Teacher learning and leadership: Of, by, and for teachers*. New York, NY: Routledge.

Lopez, S. H. (2006). Emotional labor and organized emotional care: Conceptualizing nursing home care work. *Work and Occupations, 33*(2), 133–160. doi:10.1177/0730888405284567

MacFarlane, K., & Lewis, P. (2012). United we stand: Seeking cohesive action in early childhood education and care. *Contemporary Issues in Early Childhood, 13*(1), 63–73.

Mallon, G. P., Agosti, J., & Dougherty, S. (2004). The breakthrough series collaborative methodology. New York, NY: National Resource Center for Foster Care

& Permanency Planning at Hunter College School of Social Work. Retrieved from nrcpfc.org/webcasts/archives/03/bsc-webcast-handout.pdf

Mevorach, M., & Miron, M. (2011). Experienced early childhood teachers as graduate students: A process of change. *Early Childhood Education Journal, 39*(1), 7–16. doi:10.1007/s10643-010-0442-9

Montgomery, A. W., Dacin, P. A., & Dacin, M. T. (2012). Collective social entrepreneurship: Collaboratively shaping social good. *Journal of Business Ethics, 111*(3), 375–388. doi:10.1007/s10551-012-1501-5

Morgan, G. (1997). Historical views of leadership. In S. L. Kagan & B. T. Bowman (Eds.), *Leadership in early care and education* (Ch. 2, pp. 9–14). Washington, DC: National Association for the Education of Young Children.

Muijs, D., Aubrey, C., Harris, A., & Briggs, M. (2004). How do they manage? A review of the research on leadership in early childhood. *Journal of Early Childhood Research,* 2(2), 157–169. doi:10.1177/1476718X04042974

Mulgan, G. (2006). The process of social innovation. *Technology, Governance, Globalization, 1*(2), 145–162. doi:10.1162/itgg.2006.1.2.145

Muntean, S., & Özkazanç-Pan, B. (2016). A gender integrative conceptualization of entrepreneurship. *New England Journal of Entrepreneurship, 18*(1), 3.

National Professional Development Center on Inclusion. (2008). *What do we mean by professional development in the early childhood field?* Chapel Hill, NC: Frank Porter Graham Child Development Institute, The University of North Carolina at Chapel Hill.

National Research Council. (2012). *The early childhood care and education workforce: Challenges and opportunities: A workshop report.* Washington, DC: National Academies Press.

Nembhard, I. M., & Edmondson, A. C. (2012). Psychological safety: A foundation for speaking up, collaboration, and experimentation in organizations. In K. S. Cameron & G. M. Spreitzer (Eds.), *The Oxford handbook of positive organizational scholarship* (pp. 490–503). New York, NY: Oxford University Press.

Newell J. M., & MacNeil, G. A. (2010). Professional burnout, vicarious trauma, secondary traumatic stress, and compassion fatigue: A review of theoretical terms, risk factors, and preventive methods for clinicians and researchers. *Best Practice in Mental Health,* 6(2), 57–68.

Office of Planning, Research and Evaluation, Administration for Children and Families, U.S. Department of Health and Human Services. (2017, March 28). Culture of Continuous Learning Project: A Breakthrough Series Collaborative for improving child care and head start quality. Washington, DC: Author. Retrieved from acf.hhs.gov/opre/resource/culture-of-continuous-learning-project-a-breakthrough-series-collaborative-for-improving-child-care-and-head-start-quality

O'Neill, S. M., Hempel, S., Lim, Y. W., Danz, M. S., Foy, R., Suttorp, M. J., . . . & Rubenstein, L. V. (2011). Identifying continuous quality improvement publications: What makes an improvement intervention "CQI"? *BMJ Quality & Safety, 20,* 1011–1019. doi:10.1136/bmjqs.2010.050880

Ospina, S., & Foldy, E. (2010). Building bridges from the margins: The work of leadership in social change organizations. *The Leadership Quarterly, 21*(2), 292–307. doi:10.1016/j.leaqua.2010.01.008

Parlakian, R. (Ed.). (2002). *Reflective supervision in practice: Stories from the field.* Washington, DC: Zero to Three.

Peterson, S. (2013). Readiness to change: Effective implementation processes for meeting people where they are. In T. Halle, A. Metz, & I. Martinez-Beck (Eds.), *Applying implementation science in early childhood programs and systems* (pp. 43–64). Baltimore, MD: Brookes.

Pianta, R., Cox, M., & Snow, K. (2007). *School readiness and the transition to kindergarten in the era of accountability*. Baltimore, MD: Brookes.

Prochaska, J. O. (2008). Decision making in the transtheoretical model of behavior change. *Medical Decision Making, 28*(6), 845–849.

Quinn, R. E., Dutton, J. E., Spreitzer, G. M., & Roberts, L. M. (2011). *Reflected best self exercise*. Ann Arbor, MI: University of Michigan Ross School of Business and Center for Positive Organizational Scholarship.

Raelin, J. (2011). From leadership-as-practice to leaderful practice. *Leadership, 7*(2), 195–211. doi:10.1177/1742715010394808

Ramgopal, P. S., Dieterle, K. P., Aviles, J., McCreedy, B., & Davis, C. F. (2009). Leadership development in the south: Where do we go from here? *Dimensions of Early Childhood, 37*(3), 33–38.

Rego, A., Sousa, F., Marques, C., & Cunha, M. P. (2012). Authentic leadership promoting employees' psychological capital and creativity. *Journal of Business Research, 65*(3), 429–437. doi:10.1016/j.jbusres.2011.10.003

Rodd, J. (1998). *Leadership in early childhood education* (2nd ed.). Sydney, Australia: Allen & Unwin.

Satkowski, C. (2009). *The next step in systems-building: Early Childhood Advisory Councils and federal efforts to promote policy alignment in early childhood*. Washington, DC: New America Foundation.

Schaack, D., Tarrant, K., Boller, K., & Tout, K. (2012). Quality rating and improvement systems: Frameworks for early care and education systems change. In S. L. Kagan & K. Kauerz (Eds.), *Early childhood systems: Transforming early learning* (pp. 71–86). New York, NY: Teachers College Press.

Senge, P. M. (2006). *The fifth discipline: The art and practice of the learning organization* (rev. ed.). New York, NY: Doubleday/Currency.

Shonkoff, J. P., & Phillips, D. A. (2000). *From neurons to neighborhoods: The science of early childhood development*. Washington, DC: National Academy Press.

Shulman, L. S., Wilson, S. M., & Hutchings, P. (2004). *The wisdom of practice: Essays on teaching, learning, and learning to teach*. San Francisco, CA: Jossey-Bass.

Smith, K., & Petersen, J. L. (2006). What is educational entrepreneurship? In F. M. Hess (Ed.), *Educational Entrepreneurship* (pp. 21–44). Cambridge, MA: Harvard Education Press.

Sprang, G., Craig, C., & Clark, J. (2011). Secondary traumatic stress and burnout in child welfare workers: A comparative analysis of occupational distress across professional groups. *Child Welfare, 90*(6), 149–168.

Stone, R. I., Reinhard, S. C., Bowers, B., Zimmerman, D., Phillips, C. D., Hawes, C., . . . & Jacobson, N. (2002). *Evaluation of the Wellspring model for improving nursing home quality*. New York, NY: Commonwealth Fund.

Stone-MacDonald, A. K., Wendell, K. B., Douglass, A., & Love, M. L. (2015). *Engaging young engineers: Teaching problem-solving skills through STEM*. Baltimore, MD: Paul H. Brookes.

Stoney, L., & Blank, S. (2011, July). Delivering quality: Strengthening the business side of early care and education. *Opportunities Exchange.* Retrieved from opportunities-exchange.org/wp-content/uploads/OpEx_IssueBrief2_BizSide-final.pdf

Stoney, L., Mitchell, A., & Warner, M. E. (2006). Smarter reform: Moving beyond single-program solutions to an early care and education system. *Journal of the Community Development Society, 37*(2), 101.

Suchman, A. L., Sluyter, D. J., & Williamson, P. R. (Eds.). (2014). *Leading change in healthcare: Transforming organizations using complexity, positive psychology and relationship-centered care.* New York, NY: Radcliffe Publishing.

Sullivan, D. R. (2009, July/August). Spreading the wealth: Leadership at all levels. *Leadership Exchange*, pp. 14–16.

Taba, S., Castle, A., Vermeer, M., Hanchett, K., Flores, D., & Caulfield, R. (1999). Lighting the path: Developing leadership in early education. *Early Childhood Education Journal, 26*(3), 173–177.

Tout, K., Cleveland, J., Li, W., Starr, R., Soli, M., & Bultinck, E. (2016). *The Parent Aware evaluation: Initial validation report.* Minneapolis, MN: Child Trends.

Tout, K., Epstein, D. J., Soli, M., & Lowe, C. (2015). *A blueprint for early care and education quality improvement initiatives: Final report.* Retrieved from childtrends.org/wp-content/uploads/2015/03/2015-07BlueprintEarlyCareandEd.pdf

Tout, K., Isner, T., & Zaslow, M. (2011). *Coaching for quality improvement: Lessons learned from quality rating and improvement systems* (Research Brief). Washington, DC: Child Trends.

Tout, K., Metz, A., & Bartley, L. (2013). Considering statewide professional development systems. In T. Halle, A. Metz, & I. Martinez-Beck (Eds.), *Applying implementation science in early childhood programs and systems* (pp. 243–268). Baltimore, MD: Brookes.

Tout, K., Starr, R., Soli, M., Moodie, S., Kirby, G., & Boller, K. (2010). *Compendium of quality rating systems and evaluations* (OPRE Report). Washington, DC: Office of Planning, Research and Evaluation, Administration for Children and Families, U.S. Department of Health and Human Services.

Uhl-Bien, M., Marion, R., & McKelvey, B. (2007). Complexity leadership theory: Shifting leadership from the industrial age to the knowledge era. *The Leadership Quarterly, 18*(4), 298–318. doi:10.1016/j.leaqua.2007.04.002

Uhl-Bien, M., & Ospina, S. (2012). *Advancing relational leadership research: A dialogue among perspectives.* Charlotte, NC: Information Age.

UMass Boston. (2016, March 3). *UMass Boston developing innovative and entrepreneurial early education leaders* [Video file]. Retrieved from youtube/u6lyGYgaV54

United Nations Conference on Trade and Development. (2011). Key aspects of entrepreneurship and innovation policy frameworks for enhancing local productive capacities. Retrieved from unctad.org/en/Docs/ciid13_en.pdf

U.S. Department of Education. (2010). *Toward the identification of features of effective professional development for early childhood educators: Literature review.* Washington, DC: Office of Planning, Evaluation and Policy Development, Policy and Program Studies Service.

Wesley, P. W., & Buysse, V. (2010). *The quest for quality: Promising innovations for early childhood programs.* Baltimore, MD: Brookes.

Whitebook, M. (1999). Child care workers: High demand, low wages. *The Annals of the American Academy of Political and Social Science, 563*(1), 146–161.

Whitebook, M., Kipnis, F., & Bellm, D. (2008). *Diversity and stratification in California's early care and education workforce.* Berkeley, CA: Center for the Study of Child Care Employment, University of California at Berkeley.

Whitebook, M., Kipnis, F., Sakai, L., & Austin, L.J.E. (2012). Early care and education leadership and management roles: Beyond homes and centers. *Early Childhood Research and Practice, 14*(1), 1–11.

Whitebook, M., Phillips, D., & Howes, C. (2014). *Worthy work, STILL unlivable wages: The early childhood workforce 25 years after the National Child Care Staffing Study.* Berkeley, CA: Center for the Study of Child Care Employment, University of California at Berkeley.

Whitebook, M., & Sakai, L. (2003). Turnover begets turnover: An examination of job and occupational instability among child care center staff. *Early Childhood Research Quarterly, 18*(3), 273–293.

Winton, P. J., & McCollum, J. A. (2008). Preparing and supporting high-quality early childhood practitioners: Issues and evidence. In P. J. Winton, J. A. McCollum, & C. Catlett (Eds.), *Practical approaches to early childhood professional development* (pp. 1–12). Washington, DC: Zero to Three.

Wise, V., & Wright, T. (2012). Critical absence in the field of educational administration: Framing the (missing) discourse of leadership in early childhood settings. *International Journal of Educational Leadership Preparation, 7*(2), n2.

Wood, E., & Bennett, N. (2000). Changing theories, changing practice: Exploring early childhood teachers' professional learning. *Teaching and Teacher Education, 16*(5/6), 635–647. doi:10.1016/S0742-051X(00)00011-1

Woodrow, C., & Busch, G. (2008). Repositioning early childhood leadership as action and activism. *European Early Childhood Education Research Journal, 16*(1), 83–93. doi:10.1080/13502930801897053

Yamada, K. (2013). *What do you do with an idea?* Seattle, WA: Compendium.

Yoo, J., Brooks, D., & Patti, R. (2007). Organizational constructs as predictors of effectiveness in child welfare interventions. *Child Welfare, 86*(1), 53–78.

Index

About the Author

Anne L. Douglass, PhD, is associate professor of early childhood education and care and founding executive director at the Institute for Early Education Leadership and Innovation at the University of Massachusetts Boston. Her teaching and research focus on child care quality improvement, professional development, leadership, policy, and family engagement. For over 2 decades, she has worked to strengthen family-centered and trauma-informed practice in early care and education settings, with a focus on organizational change, leadership, and resilience. She studies relational organizational systems and their capacity to create the conditions that enable high-quality teaching and family-centered practice. Her leadership work is dedicated to the design of programs, systems, and policies that support individual and collective leadership for quality improvement and innovation among early educators. Her work has been funded by the U.S. Departments of Education and Health and Human Services, as well as by private foundations including The Boston Foundation. Her research has been published in a wide range of academic journals and books, and she presents nationally and internationally at academic, policy, and professional meetings. She brings almost 20 years of expertise as an urban early educator to this work, as a teacher, administrator, family child care owner and educator, and quality improvement coach and mentor. Her experience as a practitioner working directly with children, families, and teachers informs her deep respect for the expertise of early educators as the drivers of transformative change in early childhood programs and the profession. She earned a PhD in social policy at the Heller School at Brandeis University, an EdM at Harvard Graduate School of Education, and a bachelor's degree in political science from Wellesley College.